T. S. Eliot

In the same series

BRECHT

SARTRE

CAMUS

GIDE

PROUST

JAMES

HISTORY OF LITERARY CRITICISM

T. S. Eliot

By GEORGES CATTAUI

translated by Claire Pace & Jean Stewart

THE MERLIN PRESS
LONDON

First published in France by
Editions Universitaires
Printed in Great Britain by
Clarke, Doble & Brendon Ltd.,
Cattedown, Plymouth

CONTENTS

INTRODUCTION vii

1. THE POET'S LIFE AND WORLD 1

2. THE EARLY POEMS 26
   FROM PRUFROCK TO GERONTION
   (1910 - 1920)

3. FROM THE WASTE LAND TO MARINA 43

4. THE SPIRITUAL POEMS 59
   FROM ASH WEDNESDAY TO FOUR QUARTETS
   (1930 - 1945)

5. THE POETIC DRAMAS 86
   FROM THE ROCK TO THE ELDER STATESMAN

6. AESTHETICS AND CRITICISM, CULTURE AND CHRISTIANITY 105

BIBLIOGRAPHY 123

INTRODUCTION

WHEN THE *Mayflower* set sail, carrying the pilgim Fathers towards the New World, she took with her part of the English spring. Its seeds bore precious fruit in virgin land; now some of these, when sown once more in their native soil, were to bring forth new species. Such is the work of T. S. Eliot. Like the anemones which, according to legend, sprang up in the Campo Santo at Pisa, where soil from Palestine had been added to the native earth, Eliot's poetry has an exotic attraction deriving from its twofold origin : it bears a perfume at once mystical and outlandish—the incense of biblical chants mingles with a transatlantic tang. Eliot might well declare, with Supervielle :

L'Amérique a donné son murmure à mon coeur.

In the early nineteenth century, two contrary yet mutually enriching poetic traditions grew up, which were to predominate in the United States. The first was that of Edgar Allan Poe—symbolist, subjective, musical (in fact truly *orphic*)—the tradition also of Baudelaire, Mallarmé and Valéry; the second was that of Walt Whitman—popular, rhetorical, humanitarian, prophetic. Eliot has shown little enthusiasm for Poe's poetry, and has declared his dislike of Whitman; yet their rival claims are harmonized in his work. His poetry has been described as music composed of images; it is also heir to that more informal manner which borders on prose, though without a hint of vulgarity.

Arnold Bennett once said of Eliot what had been hinted at concerning Henry James, that he was more European than the Europeans and had kept nothing of his native America. I consider, on the contrary, that we can fully understand Eliot only if we trace the links that join him to his background—to Harvard, the old-established university, to those austere intellectual dynasties from which he sprang. Perhaps we should go right back to his English ancestors, whose line he has caused to flourish again; not only to the Pilgrim Fathers who left England in the time of Charles I through loyalty to their religion, but also to the country squires to whose estates Eliot paid a pilgrimage and, even more remote, the Norman knights who may have come from France—the Elyots whose bold and militant spirit lives again in their descendant.[1]

Only an American springing from old stock could achieve so natural a synthesis of the Mediterranean and British traditions; his work blends Puritan rigour with Catholic universality, and joins to its evocation of old Breton legends the plaintive lamentations of Israel. Eliot is a typical fruit of that branch of the Bostonian line which produced Irving Babbitt, Santayana, Paul Elmer More and Henry James. In his work the critical instinct fuses with the creative impulse, and attains the heights of poetry; he gives a poetic value to mediaeval scholastic terminology. He recalls one of those enlightened American collectors who have the art of juxtaposing, without incongruity, their heterogeneous treasures, bringing out unsuspected affinities.

We might say that modern American poetry was, in a sense, born in London about 1914, amongst the group of exiled American poets who were strongly influenced by the French Symbolists. W. B. Yeats declared, when guest of honour in 1914 of the American review *Poetry,* that America suffered from being too remote, not from England but from Paris, since it was from Paris that almost all great artistic and literary influences had come, from Chaucer's time to the present day. Thanks to Eliot, Boston is no longer such a long way from

[1] Does he not number three Normans among those who have influenced him most strongly—Baudelaire, Flaubert and Gourmont?

Paris. To grasp the significance of Eliot's second journey to Europe, in 1913—for him at once an uprooting and a liberation; to gain an insight into this "break" with his native America, with his memories of childhood on the banks of the Mississippi, with the echo of children's voices in the woods, with the recollections of Harvard and the square white houses of Boston; to understand all this, we must read Henry James's short story *Europe*. Then we may realize why the young Eliot felt compelled to make such violently dogmatic assertions; he had to combat familiar ghosts. If he had not felt the need to affirm his preference for order, in reaction to an excessively vague unitarianism or the extravagances of a transcendental romanticism, his true genius—which was one day to flower in the *Four Quartets*—would have drawn him imperceptibly towards Emerson, whose sole mistake was to have believed that nature can free us from the past.[2] Indeed, Goethe seems to have foreseen the author of *Four Quartets* when he extols "the fortunate man who had enough perseverance and self-sacrifice to assimilate tradition entirely and yet preserve enough energy and courage to give his original nature an autonomous development."[3] Aiming at an eventual classicism, Eliot has in his poetry exploited the rarest hidden potentialities of the English language, controlling the complex structure of sense and sound without neglecting the advantages of direct, brief and startling simplicity. If and when we stop dividing the world's literature into horizontal and vertical compartments, we shall have a clearer estimate of Eliot's position; his poetry is like a black diamond prism, reflecting myriad rays.

There has been much discussion of the Eliot "myth": what writer is without his legend? Goethe in his old age came to consider himself as mythical; the different stages of his life seemed transparent to him, and some of his works unfamiliar, like the dead skins sloughed by a snake. The same thing is no doubt

[2] M. A. Frederick sees in Eliot the synthesis between puritanism, which exaggerates *transcendance,* and the unitarianism of Emerson and R. W. Trine, which stresses *immanence.*

[3] Quoted by E. R. Curtius, *Essais sur la Littérature Européenne.*

true of Eliot. He has created a form capable of expressing a moment of civilization; he has become, almost unawares, the voice of his age. In expressing himself, he interprets his time.

Eliot expresses our common discontents with an accent at once very personal and very traditional. His "triumphs of Death", his Lenten litanies, his legendary Dantesque world, lit by a weird and spectral glow, evoke the burnt, barbaric landscapes of the Ferrarese school of painters—the glassy deserts and rocky wildernesses of Cosimo Tura, the petrified world of Francesco del Cossa, the spiky, metallic trees of Ercole de' Roberti. His incisive precision is the result of spiritual discipline, of an acute self-awareness. And the blinding metaphysical light plays its part; it becomes "an original force striving towards material representation of its own symbol". Eliot's poetry resounds with the sudden explosion of compressed energies. It renders the familiar strange, and the strange familiar. His work as a whole comprises *one single poem*. And our concern here is with his work as a whole, not with the poetry of particular isolated passages. In this way, Eliot, self-effacing as he is, has given us the basic tone of personal emotion that no biography could possibly provide.

1. *The Poet's Life and World*

> *We are born with the dead:*
> *See, they return, and bring us with them.*
> *The moment of the rose and the moment*
> *of the yew-tree*
> *Are of equal duration. (Little Gidding).*

THE WHOLE of Eliot's life, and the whole of his work, consist of the exploration of, and search for, the past brought to remembrance, of a pilgrimage to "the source of the longest river." Eliot believes that all poetry has for its point of departure the emotions experienced by a human being in his relations with himself, with others and with his environment; yet he himself has remained extremely unforthcoming about the significant events of his own life, and his reticence has hardly facilitated the task of his biographers. With Eliot, we are justified in looking for the "figure in the carpet", that hidden but always discernible pattern which Henry James described. His poetry must be our guide in tracing the outline of his individual features. He has suffered from the efforts of too many enthusiasts, perfidiously seeking traces of a confession between the lines of a poem. "I am used to having cosmic significances, which I never suspected, extracted from my work (such as it is) by enthusiastic persons at a distance; and to being informed that something which I meant seriously is '*vers de société*', and to having my personal biography reconstructed from passages which I got out of books, or which I invented out of nothing because they sounded well; and to having my biography invariably ignored in what I did write from personal experience; so that in consequence I am inclined to believe that people are mistaken about Shakespeare just in proportion to the relative superiority of Shakespeare to myself."[1] Let us endeavour to steer clear of this twofold peril.

[1] *Selected Essays*, p. 127. Faber, 1944.

We must devote a few words to Eliot's genealogy, for it is of special interest: he owes certain of his gifts to his Puritan heredity, and his work contains many allusions to his ancestors. These mute forebears find frequent expression in the words of their distant descendant; poetry is sometimes recollection, sometimes prophecy.

Thomas Stearns Eliot was born on September 26th 1888, in the old city of St Louis, which had for a long time been the capital of French Louisiana before becoming that of the State of Missouri. He was the youngest of the seven sons of Henry Ware Eliot (1843-1919) and Charlotte Chauncy Stearns (1843-1929), daughter of a Boston tradesman, whose ancestor Isaac Stearns had been one of the pioneers of the colony. Her husband Henry Ware Eliot, after studying at Washington University, became a partner in, then President of, the Hydraulic Press Brick Company. But the poet's ancestors came from further afield; they were of Norman stock. We find Elyots successively in Somerset and Devon—above all in East Coker, where lived Sir Thomas Elyot, author of *A Boke named the Governour*, a few lines of which are quoted in *Four Quartets*. About 1670 Andrew Eliot (1627-1704), a cordwainer by trade, left the village of East Coker to emigrate to America. He settled in Massachusetts, where his name is recorded in the register of the First Church of Beverly. He was a witness at the Salem witch trials, but afterwards publicly recanted, and never forgave himself for having committed this error of justice. His numerous descendants played a prominent role in the history of New England. The Rev. Andrew Eliot (1718-1778) of Boston was violently opposed to the Episcopalians; he was elected President of Harvard, but refused to abandon his parish. The Eliots of Boston, strictly orthodox Presbyterians, were converted to Unitarianism, a sect which, while discarding the essence of Christian dogma, seeks to reconcile Platonism with the wisdom of the Gospels.

The poet's grandfather, William Greenleaf Eliot, who came to St Louis to found the first Unitarian chapel there in 1834, would have been amazed if anyone had predicted that his grandson would one day adopt most of the traditions represented by the town of St Louis, founded by the French under Louis XIV—royalist, Latin, Catholic traditions which recall Ignatius Loyola rather than Calvin, Thomas Aquinas rather than Emerson.

A poet's childhood is always particularly fascinating. We should like to know more about Eliot's childhood, but he has been more than discreet concerning his early years. We know that as a boy he enjoyed going on long expeditions with his friends to the chalk cliffs where you could find fossil shells; that he loved to listen to the sound of the big river, the dark Mississippi which he has never forgotten. Perhaps his mother used to tell him the story of the martyrdom of Savonarola; she had written a long dramatic poem about it.[2] He was not yet ten years old when he started his literary career; as a schoolboy he founded, edited (and distributed to the members of his family) a periodical entitled *Fireside*. He wrote a *Life of George Washington* in ten lines; evidently he already had the gift of conciseness.

According to Eliot's own recollections, up to the age of twelve he was, like most boys of that age, attracted only by "martial and sanguinary" poetry such as the Border Ballads. Then all of a sudden he lost his liking for that kind of verse, indeed for every form of poetry, for two or three years. The only pleasure he derived from Shakespeare was "the pleasure of being commended for reading him."[3] But when at the age of about fourteen he happened to see an extract from Fitzgerald's paraphrase of Omar Khayyàm, he had the overwhelming sensation of entering an unknown universe, a whole new way of feeling, revealed to him by the poem. "It was like a sudden conversion; the world appeared anew, painted with bright, delicious and painful colours. Thereupon I took the usual adolescent course with Byron, Shelley, Keats, Rossetti and Swinburne. I take this attitude to have persisted until my nineteenth or twentieth

[2] This work, which was published in London by Cobden Sanderson in 1926, with a preface by T. S. Eliot, is "steeped in the doctrines of Schleiermacher, Emerson and Herbert Spencer."

[3] *The Use of Poetry and the Use of Criticism,* p. 33.

year. Being a period of rapid assimilation, the end may not know the beginning, so different may the taste become. Like the first period of childhood, it is one beyond which I dare say many people never advance; so that such taste for poetry as they retain in later life is only a sentimental memory of the pleasures of youth, and is probably entwined with all our other sentimental retrospective feelings."[4]

Baudelaire observed, comparing the mature works of an artist with his personality as a child, that "genius is only childhood clearly formulated, endowed with adult and effective means of expression". And so "some childish joy or sorrow, enormously magnified by an exquisite sensibility, becomes in the grown man, even though he may not be aware of it, the origin of a work of art". We should like to know Eliot's childhood impressions, for we would surely discover in them "the seed of the grown man's strange visions, indeed of his genius". Baudelaire is right to emphasize that the significance of stories about an artist's childhood has never been adequately stressed. And he continues: "Often, when studying works of art—not in their material aspects, which are easily understood, but in the spirit which pervades them, the atmosphere which they create, the spiritual light or shadow which they shed upon our hearts—I have experienced as it were a vision of the childhood of the artists who created them."[5]

As Eliot points out, "only a part of an author's imagery comes from his reading. It comes from the whole of his sensitive life since early childhood. Why, for all of us, out of all that we have heard, seen, felt, in a lifetime, do certain images recur, charged with emotion, rather than others? The song of one bird" (the hermit-thrush) "the leap of one fish, at a particular place and time, the scent of one flower" (lilac or hyacinth) "an old woman on a German mountain path, six ruffians seen through an open window playing cards at night at a small French railway junction where there was a water-mill:[6] such

[4] *The Use of Poetry and the Use of Criticism,* p. 33.
[5] Baudelaire, *Les Paradis Artificiel, Le Génie Enfant,* p. 317.
[6] See *The Journey of the Magi.*

memories may have symbolic value, but of what we cannot tell, for they come to represent the depths of feeling into which we cannot peer."[7]

After studying first at Smith Academy, St Louis, and then at Milton Academy Mass., Eliot enrolled at Harvard in 1906, at the age of eighteen. It seemed to him rather like entering the "ancestral home", so many members of his family had distinguished themselves there. Cambridge, where the University stands, recalls its English Alma Mater and everything that Eliot holds dear. Yet his first reaction was one of revolt against his surroundings. His earliest poems are full of gibes at the Bostonian mentality, at the *Boston Evening Transcript,* or "my maiden aunt Miss Helen Slingsby", or Prufrock's inhibitions. For, as the American critic Van Wyck Brooks has mischievously pointed out, we can discover in Eliot's work nearly all the tastes and attitudes which characterized earlier Bostonians: Bostonian royalism and Anglo-Catholicism, a liking for Donne, Laforgue and Gourmont, an interest in Dante, the Bhagavad-Gita, Elizabethan dramatists and poets—all the constituents of Babbitt's and Santayana's classicism.

This young American seems to have been born weary of living. In *Preludes,* written about 1910, Eliot constantly evokes the tedium of Puritan provincial life, the gloom of the winter evening which

> "   settles down
> With smell of steak in passageways"

while

> "The showers beat
> On broken blinds and chimney-pots,
> And at the corner of the street
> A lonely cab-horse steams and stamps . . ."

The poem is full of such images of sordidness and desolation. As a student, Eliot must often have roamed through the suburban streets as evening drew on, noting "the newspapers from vacant lots"; he must often have seen the office workers hurry-

[7] *The Use of Poetry and the Use of Criticism,* p. 148.

ing in the morning towards the "early coffee-stands", and have visited the dingy lodgings of some ambitious young man who was, like himself, "impatient to assume the world". The yellow fog that filled the street and "rubbed its back upon the window-panes" (in *The Love Song of J. Alfred Prufrock*) might equally well be that of London or Oxford as that of Boston; what pin-points the scene is the picture of "lonely men in shirtsleeves leaning out of windows" and smoking their pipes. But Eliot was destined to carry away, too, very different memories of his native land. He had a great passion for the sea, which he has always kept. He was an enthusiastic sailor, and memories of his sailing expeditions have persisted; when at the age of nearly sixty he wrote of the "consecrated places" in his memory, of those in New England he chose the Dry Salvages, three rocks off Cape Ann which provided him with the material for a powerful allegory. All Eliot's poems are to a certain extent a sailor's poems, making constant use of maritime metaphors. He is one of that admirable race of men which, on both sides of the Atlantic, has never forgotten its links with the sea; its finest expressions—from *The Ancient Mariner* to *The Dry Salvages* by way of *Moby Dick*—are evocations of the life of the ocean. So it is not at all surprising to find so many maritime terms in Eliot's verse: it is full of the "lost sea-smell", foam, atolls, seaweed, mermaids, bell-buoys, sea-mist, currents, the Gulf Stream, reefs, the cry of gulls flying against the wind, cargoes of tin and the Cornish surf; and also—from Apollinax to Phlebas:

"the old man of the sea,
Hidden under coral islands
Where worried bodies of drowned men drift down in the green silence."

When they settled in Missouri, the Eliots jealously preserved their links with Boston; yet it was only when he grew to adult-hood that Eliot realized that he had always remained a child of New England when living in the South and equally a child of the South when living in New England. When he was sent to school in Massachusetts, he lost his Southern accent, but did not acquire a Boston accent in its place. He even wrote later: "In New England I missed the long dark river, the ailanthus trees, the flaming cardinal birds, the high limestone bluffs where we searched for fossil shell-fish; in Missouri I missed the firtrees, the bay and golden-rod, the song-sparrows, the red granite and the blue sea of Massachusetts."[8] Gradually the young man from St Louis came to love the Boston of his forebears. Although all his instincts were opposed to the intellectual tradition of Franklin, Emerson and Trine, yet at Harvard he discovered a tradition of Classical humanist learning from which he was to profit greatly. Henry Adams had shown the way when he rediscovered the sculpture of Chartres and became a disciple of Aquinas. Dantean scholarship had been revived by Charles Eliot Norton and Charles Grandgent in their essays on the *Divine Comedy*. At Harvard Eliot studied under Irving Babbit with whom, as with Paul Elmer More,

> ". . . the French influence is traceable in their devotion to ideas and their interest in problems of art as problems which exist and can be handled apart from their relations to the critic's private temperament."[9]

Babbitt's lectures (which were later published under the title *Masters of Modern French Criticism*) taught Eliot to make sharp and clearly defined distinctions and then to use these as tools of character and will—a discipline which he contrasts with that of Bergson. Eliot was not to be satisfied with studying Western philosophy from Aristotle to Bradley. He was attracted by Hinduism, by the *Vedas, Upanishads* and above all by the *Bhagavad-Gita,* which he has always considered, together with the *Divine Comedy,* the greatest of all philosophic poems.[10]

Eliot's verse is pervaded by a nostalgia for the Old World

[8] Preface to E. A. Mowrer's *This American World,* 1928.

[9] *The Sacred Wood,* p. 39.

[10] Eliot studied Sanscrit and Pali, in order to gain a deeper understanding of Indian culture.

and for tradition—a nostalgia peculiar to New England. And there is also a certain sense of spaciousness, of wide horizons, as well as of precise particular places, with which all American literature seems to be imbued. One of the most remarkable achievements of American culture is the creation of a distinctive literary and poetic idiom. From Twain to Faulkner, and from Frost to Eliot, the principal craftsmen of this way of speech, although they have often been cosmopolitan-minded, have always been innovators, who could raise a mundane idiom to poetic heights, and give an incantatory magic to the everyday conversation of the man in the street.

The tendency towards concentrated, cryptic and rhythmic language derives from Melville as well as from Henry James. This new form of expression may often be esoteric, but it nevertheless retains its colloquial flavour. And in its turn, through the theatre, it had considerable influence on the sensibility and way of speech of the general public; for the character of a nation, we must not forget, is to a great extent the creation of its poets. Thus Eliot, although he left Boston for London, has, through his poetic genius and his "auditory imagination", contributed to the formation of the accent and vocabulary of tomorrow's American *élite*.

When Eliot began writing poetry at the age of nearly twenty, he might well have modelled himself on Yeats, who already enjoyed a considerable reputation, although his early manner—that of the Celtic revival—was far from the perfection of his later poems, whose originality Eliot fully recognized. Then, around 1908, Eliot felt that the kind of poetry he needed in order to teach him "the use of (his) own voice" did not exist in English at all, and was only to be found in French. "The taste of an adolescent writer is intense but narrow, it is determined by personal needs."[11] Eliot was looking for masters who would gradually reveal to him the kind of poetry that he himself was destined to write; such masters he found in the French Symbolists and those writers called, rightly or wrongly, the inventers of *vers libre*, especially Laforgue and Corbière. In their

[11] "The Poetry of W. B. Yeats", *Purpose, July-December,* 1940.

work not only were scansion, rhythm and rhyme (until then rigid and stereotyped) liberated, but a whole new idiom was created, close to the spoken language, to the natural everyday speech of a man concerned to express the mood and temper of his time.

It was in a student magazine, *The Harvard Advocate,* that Eliot published his first poems at the age of twenty. He himself said later that the form he adopted in 1908 and 1909 was directly derived from his study of Laforgue as well as from the Elizabethan drama in its later phase. Arthur Symons' book, *The Symbolist Movement in Literature,* had provided him with the predestined revelation of Laforgue, Rimbaud, Verlaine and Corbière.[12] Eliot felt for this writer a sense of profound kinship, of singular personal intimacy. The sensation was overwhelming; he was "seized by his first passion of this sort, and transformed, almost metamorphosed, in less than a few weeks, from a jumble of secondhand sentiments into *a person.*" Contact with Laforgue was for him a formative instrument like a personal relationship. Eliot's work reveals that search for reconciliation between extreme strictness and extreme liberty which, according to Valéry, first appeared in France between the Parnassians and the Symbolists; it has "the effect of blending the architectural structure of one group with the music of the other." "An extreme degree of refinement . . . always leads to a kind of suicide; in its striving for supreme simplicity, it dies . . ."

The student-poet, while absorbed in his efforts to "distinguish the elements implicit" in Laforgue's poetry, was at the same time creating his own poetic style. He described later[13] how a poet at the outset of his career might feel a pronounced sympathy for a certain type of poetry—that of Laforgue and some other French poets for instance—through which his own talents might develop.

[12] "Reflections on Contemporary Poetry", *The Egoist,* July 1919, p. 39 cf. also Peter Quennell, "Baudelaire and the Symbolists", *Criterion,* January 1930, p. 357.

[13] *A Garland for John Donne, Harvard,* 1931, p. 6.

Admittedly Eliot could not at that stage distinguish between a natural affinity and one that resulted from his habit of endowing the poet he was reading with his own sensibility. The fact remains that he found in Laforgue's *Complaintes* a living language and themes which answered his own requirements, his uncertainties, his taste for irony, his discretion, his refinement, his "dandyism".[14]

Eliot has not considered his first poems worthy of preservation, since they comprise only notes "in the margin of Laforgue"; *On a Portrait, Nocturne, Humoresque, Spleen*—the very titles reveal his debt to the Symbolists. Corbière's influence succeeded that of Laforgue. Eliot read *Les Amours Jaunes* and was fascinated by the mixture of humour and realism, transfigured by the poet's caustic tone, his abrupt style and undemonstrative manner. This "patchwork assortment" had for him an elusive, unfamiliar flavour; he liked its prosody, "whispered rather than sung", its rejection of romantic eloquence and hackneyed themes in favour of the unpretentious, intimate and direct tone of folksong and ballads—laments, lullabies, refrains and litanies. What impressed him above all was the sense of the sea which pervaded Corbière's poems; their author, that "mongrel mixture of Creole and Breton", was himself "bitter and salty" like his beloved ocean.

More and more now, a stranger in his own land, in the gloomy Boston of the Cabots and Lowells, Eliot felt the urge to go abroad. So he travelled; he visited France, England and Germany; he followed courses at their universities, grew to know their poetry, studied the precepts of their philosophers; he made a pilgrimage to Ravenna. In 1910 he was at the Sorbonne; but he needed to perfect his French. He was fortunate enough to have as his tutor, guide and inspiration Alain-Fournier, who gave him private lessons for several months. Surely this meeting between the author of *Le Grand Meaulnes* and the future author of *Four Quartets* must have been predestined; both were occupied with the search for the lost

[14] On the influence of Laforgue see E. J. H. Greene, *T. S. Eliot et la France,* Boirin, Paris, 1951.

arcadia of childhood. Alain-Fournier revealed to Eliot the work of Dostoievsky and Gide, Claudel's earliest plays, and his *Connaissance de l'Est*. He also introduced him to his brother-in-law Jacques Rivière, whose advice Eliot sought about undertaking an ambitious academic project.[15] The poet was later to expatiate on his good fortune in discovering Paris, as a youth, in 1910, when the *Nouvelle Revue Française* was really new and the *Cahiers de la Quinzaine* were appearing in their austere grey-paper covers, and Bergson was lecturing weekly to crowded audiences at the College de France; Paris was the whole of the past and the whole of the future, both aspects combined in a perfect present.

Now famous, but still faithful, Eliot adds that if this was what France meant to him, it might be through some fortunate accident; but it was no accident that had taken him to Paris, since for several years past France had meant for him, above all else, poetry.[16] Laforgue and Corbière were not the only French writers to influence Eliot. He later came under the spell of Verlaine, Laurent Tailhade, Rimbaud, Baudelaire, and—surprisingly—Théophile Gautier, whose *Emaux et Camées* provided him with a model of incisive, compact and disciplined metre. Among prose writers, finally, he greatly admired Stendhal, Flaubert, Rémy de Gourmont, Charles Maurras, Julien Benda, and, later, Maritain. ". . . Immature poets imitate; mature poets steal; bad poets deface what they take and good poets make it into something better, or at least different."[17]

Eliot himself has experienced both stages; though he may pillage freely, what he takes he transforms into something absolutely his own.

At this stage Eliot was a slight young man, fair, pale and shy, with a slender neck and a Gioconda smile, as his friends later described him.[18] Above all, he already possessed the deter-

[15] *Rencontre.* La Nouvelle Revue Française (special number in honour of Jacques Rivière) 1925, p. 657.

[16] "What France means to you", T. S. Eliot's answer in *La France Libre,* June 15th 1944.

[17] *The Sacred Wood,* p. 125.

[18] Wyndham Lewis, Clive Bell, Virginia Woolf.

mination, the firmness of purpose, the ascetic taste and preference for what is difficult, the desire to "cultivate his difference from others" which were to make him not only a great artist, but also an authoritative guide to the hesitant and perplexed. He was then still rather reticent and to overcome his shyness he took boxing and dancing lessons. Clive Bell speaks of his studied preciosity of language.

In a deliberate isolation, which had a touch of Baudelairean "dandyism", the New England aristocrat showed heroic concentration; he subdued the stirring of instinct and practised an ascetic cult of the artificial. If he "wore out his substance in consuming self-communion", as Laforgue says, if, with a certain provocativeness, he alienates our sympathies, it is because he has a horror of the common herd—yet he is always "courteous to the ill-favoured". "There is never a false smile in the expressions he uses."

In 1911 Eliot returned to Harvard to prepare his doctoral thesis on *Meinung's Gegenstandstheorie considered in relation to Bradley's Theory of Knowledge* . . . (he now confesses that he finds his youthful work unreadable). The following three years were as good as lost so far as poetry is concerned; not content with being a metaphysician, logician and psychologist, Eliot studied philology, learned Sanskrit and Pali, and finally, in 1913, gave a course of lectures on philosophy. Later he declared that a poet who was also a philosopher seemed to him, whatever Valéry's opinion might be, as fabulous a monster as the unicorn. It is none the less true that for the future author of the *Quartets,* though he rejected didactic philosophy, abstract thought was always to be of great importance.

In 1914 Eliot left on a scholarship for Marburg, to make a fuller study of Husserl's philosophy. On the outbreak of war, the aspiring philosopher came to England and entered Merton College, Oxford. Here he became absorbed in the study of Aristotle and the Greek philosophers; here he discovered Bradley's *Principles of Logic*. In 1915 he married a young Englishwoman, Vivienne Haigh, and therefore had to find a job. For a meagre salary, he took up a post at High Wycombe

Grammar School, to teach French, mathematics, history, geography, art—and swimming.

* *

During this period Eliot made the acquaintance, in London, of Wyndham Lewis, James Joyce and Ezra Pound. Pound encouraged him, and showed him his own true genius by publishing his first collection of poems : *Prufrock and Other Observations,* in July 1917.[19] In 1915, while war was raging, Eliot had been introduced into the Imagist group, which included, besides Pound, F. S. Flint, Richard Aldington (who later left the group) and the Belgian poet Jean de Bosschère. Their views were expressed in the review *The Egoist.* Later Eliot summed up their aims and achievements thus :

> "The accomplishment of the Imagist movement in verse seems to me, in retrospect, to have been critical rather than creative; and as criticism, very important. I am not thinking only of such work as Mr Flint's studies of contemporary French poetry, of the importance of the views of Rémy de Gourmont, or even of the more philosophical theories of T. E. Hulme as expressed in his conversation (for his influence in print belongs to a later period); but also of the Imagist poetry itself, of which only a small residue is now readable. The only poet and critic who survived Imagism to develop in a larger way was Mr Pound, who, as literary critic alone, has been probably the greatest literary influence of this century up to the present time."[20]

It was Pound who in 1917 suggested the title for the first collection of Eliot's writings : *Prufrock and Other Observations.* It was Pound, too, who persuaded him to settle in England.

[19] These had first appeared in little magazines—*Others, Blast, Little Review, Poetry.* Eliot had also published, while still a student, a philosophical article in *The Harvard Advocate,* as well as critical essays in *The International Journal of Ethics*; and, above all, in *The New Statesman* of March 1917 his "Reflections on Vers Libre" which have lost none of their interest.

[20] "A Commentary", *The New Criterion,* July 1937, p. 668.

One of Eliot's reasons for leaving America was probably a sense of the "starved environment" that had surrounded Hawthorne, Poe, and Whitman: "Their world was thin; it was not corrupt enough. Worst of all it was secondhand; it was not original and self-dependent".[21]

Soon afterwards, thanks to Pound, Eliot discovered the Italian Trecento poets, Cavalcanti, Guinicelli, Cino, as well as the Provençal troubadours; he grew to know Dante's work intimately and to esteem it ever more highly. He even borrowed from the *Divine Comedy* verses which served as *leitmotiv* in *Ash Wednesday, Animula* and *The Waste Land*. In his essay on Dante (1929) Eliot defined with admirable clarity the reasons for his admiration. The most important factor, he considers is the "coalescence" of a set of images corresponding to a given state of mind. Confronted with the collapse of the traditional discursive forms (such as those of Shelley) Eliot wanted to go on beyond the pure impressionism of the Imagists, and found a new means of composition in this association of images which seem at first sight heterogeneous.[22]

In 1917 Eliot began, and then abandoned, the publication of *Aeldrop and Appleplex,* in which, in imitation of *Bouvard et Pécuchet,* he provides an examination of contemporary society; its ironic humour later found a place in his poetry. He had not yet, however, developed an admiration for Mallarmé, who was to play such an important role in the later development of the poet of *Four Quartets*. He found the tone of *Divagations* irritating, and its "laborious opacity" seemed to him, besides Rimbaud's prose, faded and dead.[23] It was through Gourmont's *Le Livre des Masques,* and Van Bever and Léautaud's *Poetes d'Aujourd'hui* that Eliot discovered contem-

[21] "American Literature", *The Athenaeum,* April 25th 1917, p. 237.

[22] This is what Eliot calls the "objective correlative". Mario Praz has drawn attention to the first mention, in the writings of Washington Allston (*Lectures on Art,* 1850), of this phrase, which he considers one of the most important keys to Eliot's inspiration. (See M. Praz, "T. S. Eliot", *L'Italia che scrive,* October 1956.)

[23] Laboulle, "T. S. Eliot and some French Poets," *Revue de Littérature Comparée,* April-June 1939, p. 389.

porary French writing. During this period he became one of the most valued members of the literary circle centred around Lady Ottoline Morrell, at her home at Garsington, near Oxford. Here he met the great men of an older generation: Yeats, George Russell ("A.E."), Masefield, Walter de la Mare, Sturge Moore, Trevelyan—as well as his contemporaries or juniors, such as D. H. Lawrence, the Sitwells, Herbert Read and Aldous Huxley.

In a poem written in French, *Mélange Adultère de Tout* (the title is taken from a poem by Corbière), Eliot has drawn a humorous self-portrait: that of an ironic cosmopolitan like Valery Larbaud's Barnabooth:

> "En Amerique, professeur;
> En Angleterre, journaliste;
> C'est à grand pas et en sueur
> Que vous suivrez à peine ma piste.
> En Yorkshire, conférencier;
> A Londres, un peu banquier,
> Vous me paierez bien la tête . . ."

Eliot was already, whatever he might say, a wise and mature man, the image of modesty, discretion and propriety, putting down roots into the English soil. Moreover, he had recently been appointed Assistant Editor of *The Egoist,* in which his most important critical essays were published between September and November 1917. Under the pseudonym of Apteryx, he published in his review, in March 1918, a revaluation of "Georgian" poetry, followed by *Wheels,* and by *A Second Cycle* —"Verse Pleasant and Unpleasant". In the spring of 1919 he started to write for *The Athenaeum,* edited by John Middleton Murry, but it was in *The Egoist* that his essays on "Tradition and the Individual Talent" appeared, while the *Times Literary Supplement* published his justly celebrated studies of Ben Jonson and Massinger, which contained a new evaluation of the Elizabethan dramatists.[24] After a while Eliot found the teaching

[24] Reprinted in T. S. Eliot, *Selected Prose,* a collection edited by John Hayward, Penguin Books, London 1953.

profession too exhausting, and therefore accepted a post with Lloyd's Bank, where he worked for eight years. Thus the most significant post-war poem, and one which heralds a new poetic era—*The Waste Land*—was written by the employee of a bank; Eliot commented (in an interview published in France) that although poetry was not much help to him in his career in the bank, the latter enabled him to write his poems, since in the evenings his mind was not obsessed by his day's work and he could lead two distinct intellectual lives simultaneously.'

* *

The United States had now joined the war, and Eliot made great efforts to enrol in the U.S. Navy. But in 1918 he was already thirty years old, and his health was suffering from many years of overwork. He was therefore rejected.

He stayed in London, and his influence on circles of young writers grew still greater. As well as a poet, he was an essayist, a moralist, an aesthetician and sociologist. His articles, which appeared in various periodicals,[25] were published in 1920 under the title of *The Sacred Wood* (an allusion to Theocritus). In Eliot's work, poet and critic are one; the critical intellect, stretched to the furthest limits of lucidity, fuses with poetic inspiration. This fusion is in the tradition of Coleridge, Wordsworth and Matthew Arnold, who were all at the same time poets and critics. Eliot brought back into English literature qualities of steadiness and seriousness. And seriousness is a quality which always makes a strong impression on the younger generation. They feel, as Joubert did, that "taste ought to be the literary conscience of the soul, and criticism its methodical application". Eliot's criticism fulfils this function, and therein lies the source of its great influence. His sincerity compels us to revise our judgment of certain poets, and of the criteria we have hitherto applied to poetry.[26] He envisages the study of

[25] Such as *The Times Literary Supplement, The Athenaeum, The Egoist, Art and Letters,* etc.

[26] cf. Desmond McCarthy, "Poetry as Criticism of Life," *Sunday Times,* December 3rd 1933.

criticism not as a series of risky conjectures but as a readaptation, enabling us to draw some conclusions about what is permanent or eternal in poetry and what is merely the expression of a period; and by discovering what changes (*how* and *why* it changes) we may be led to apprehend what does not change.

Of the poets who have "proceeded to the expansion of reality" (and it is with these poets that Eliot is concerned), he considers Dante the greatest. Not only did he take the *Divine Comedy* as a model for his own verse, but he also put Dante scholarship in his debt by superseding the impressionistic and fragmentary interpretations of such critics at Benedetto Croce.

All these influences combined in the composition of that masterpiece, *The Waste Land.* Eliot apparently conceived the idea of the poem on a visit to Provence—near the Roman ruins of La Turbie—and wrote it as Lausanne, in 1920:

"By the waters of Leman I sat down and wept."

The poem did not appear in volume form until 1922—the same year as Joyce's *Ulysses.* Eliot takes pleasure in recalling that Ezra Pound, through his critical perception and mastery of prosody, helped "to turn *The Waste Land* from a jumble of good and bad passages into a poem";[27] for this reason the poem is dedicated to him, with a quotation from Dante: *il miglior fabbro.*

It has been said that this poem dealt a mortal blow to Romanticism, and that it is the source of all modern poetry. Indeed, since the publication of Wordsworth's *Lyrical Ballads* in 1798, no poem had excited such controversy in England. Yet its author was known only to the *avant-garde,* and had time for writing only in his scanty leisure hours, for he was still working in the City.

During this time, Eliot must have frequented the Cannon Street Hotel, to which he refers in *The Waste Land*: business men passing through London would forgather here, in the

[27] *Purpose,* April-June 1938, pp. 92-93.

heart of the City. Thus he might well have come across such exotic figures as "Mr Eugenides, the Smyrna merchant" as well as the war profiteers, the "Bradford millionaires". Coming home from the bank, "at the violet hour", Eliot would take the Underground at Moorgate station, which is also mentioned in the poem. In the heart of this old part of London, then the financial centre of the Empire, stood the Babylonian buildings from which arose the Biblical lamentation of the typist. Eliot's fondness for contrasts took him from the East End to Richmond or Kew. He would visit the docks of Poplar one day, and the next would go to Greenwich, where Elizabeth met Leicester.

In 1922, an outstanding year in his career, Eliot founded, with the encouragement of Lady Rothermere, the review *The Criterion,* of which he became editor and through which he exercised for seventeen years an authority similar to that of Jacques Rivière and Jean Paulhan on the *Nouvelle Revue Française*. In 1925 he was at last able to leave Lloyd's Bank to join the publishing firm of Faber and Gwyer (now Faber and Faber); he became a director in 1929, and has always shown himself receptive towards *avant-garde* poetry while upholding Classical traditions. And in 1926 he was chosen to deliver the Clark Lectures at Cambridge.

> "It is my experience that toward middle age a man has three choices: to stop writing altogether, to repeat himself with perhaps an increasing skill of virtuosity, or by taking thought to adapt himself to middle age and find a different way of working."[28]

This was, no doubt, Eliot's frame of mind after completing *The Waste Land*. And in fact he wrote hardly any verse between 1922 and 1925; he published only *The Hollow Men,* which is a recapitulation, in a different key, of earlier themes. Near the end of the poem, however, occur the final phrases of the Lord's Prayer, and these murmured liturgical words have

[28] "The Poetry of W. B. Yeats", *Purpose,* July-December 1940. Reprinted in Hayward, op. cit., pp. 197-205. This was originally delivered as the first annual Yeats Lecture to the Friends of the Irish Academy at the Abbey Theatre, Dublin, June 30, 1940.

an overwhelming effect. It may well be that Eliot was influenced by Maritain, whom he read in 1925. Whereas the claims of poetry are often considered by poets to be contrary to those of religion, and a reverence for dogma, ethical teaching and religious observances is seen as an obstacle to the creative instinct, Eliot felt, on the contrary, that religion could only further the free flowering of his personality. He therefore needed considerable humility to renounce his ego, thus allowing (as Maritain This was not easily achieved. For, as he says in *Little Gidding,* describes it) religious experience to strengthen, harmonize and illuminate in him the spiritual experience of poetic creation. every poem is

> ... an epitaph. And any action
> Is a step to the block, to the fire, down the sea's throat ...

Eliot was not yet thirty when, inspired by a description of the last days of the poet Fitzgerald,[29] he gave his Gerontion these disillusioned words:

> "Here I am, an old man in a dry month,
> Being read to by a boy, waiting for rain ..."

And sadly he recalls wasted time—all the acts of courage he never accomplished, all the sordid mean actions he has witnessed. Then suddenly, whether from presentiment or desire, he demands a "sign"—from the Word "unable to speak a word", a lifegiving word.

* *

In 1927, having lived in England for thirteen years, Eliot, at the age of 39, became a British citizen. More significantly, in the same year he joined the Anglican church, or, as he prefers to call it, "the Catholic Church in England". This religious development naturally finds expression in his poetry. But since

[29] Matthiessen has noted this recollection of Benson's biography of Fitzgerald, and also a possible reminiscence of *The Education of Henry Adams.*

his verse does not spring spontaneously from his impressions, but ripens slowly after long deliberation, the religious influx increased only gradually, reaching its full expression in *Ash Wednesday*. From that time on, the once irreverent Eliot is more Christian than Baudelaire; against the latter's spirit of rebellion, the poet of *Murder in the Cathedral* sets the solitude of the soldier, the priest and the saint. Eliot, following Stendhal's advice, seeks to appear unemotional, "dry". The *Ariel* Poems, which appeared between 1927 and 1930, give a hint of his religious beliefs, especially *Journey of the Magi, A Song for Simeon* and *Animula*. (The *Journey* was inspired by a sermon of Lancelot Andrewes, of which Eliot quotes a few lines as *exordium* to the poem. The verses also reveal the influence of St John Perse's *Anabase,* which Eliot translated at about this time and which was published in 1930.)

One of Eliot's most "heterogeneous", unexpected poems is *Sweeney Agonistes,* which was published in 1932 (although two fragments had appeared in 1926 and 1927). As Williamson has observed,[30] it contains the structural elements of an Aristophanic comedy, with the intervention of the Eumenides—a conception which occurs nowhere else in Eliot's work, not even in *The Family Reunion,* since there the whole tone is quite different. But the style of *Sweeney* belongs to his early manner, where the mixture of Classical allusions and music-hall rhymes seems less incongruous than the later amalgams. It has been pointed out that certain rhythms in *Sweeney Agonistes* recur in *The Cocktail Party,* in which another Greek legend—that of Alcestis—is transposed to drawing-room comedy.

* *

In 1932 Eliot was appointed for one year to the Chair of Poetry at Harvard, founded in memory of Charles Eliot Norton. Thus after eighteen years' absence Eliot returned to his native Massachusetts; but his affection for New England was sorely

[30] cf. S. Williamson, *A Reader's Guide to T. S. Eliot,* New York, 1953.

tried. On his journey from Montreal, he passed through the "beautiful desolate country of Vermont". He wrote:

> "These hills had once, I suppose, been covered with primeval forest; the forest was razed to make sheep pastures for the English settlers; now the sheep are gone, and most of the descendants of the settlers; and a new forest appeared blazing with the melancholy glory of October maple and beech and birch scattered among the ever-greens; and after this procession of scarlet and gold and purple wilderness you descend to the sordor of the half-dead mill-towns of southern New Hampshire and Massachusetts. It is not necessarily those lands which are the most fertile or most favoured in climate that seem to me the happiest, but those in which a long struggle of adaptation between man and his environment has brought out the best qualities of both; in which the landscape has been moulded by numerous generations of one race, and in which the landscape in turn has modified the race to its own character. And those New England mountains seemed to me to give evidence of a human success so meagre and transitory as to be more desperate than the desert."[31]

But for Eliot's poetry this return to the land of his youth proved to be fruitful. It was like an influx of past into present, the recollection of places in New England and Virginia, of the rocky coast of Maine, the "flowering Judas", the "scent of dogwood and chestnut". Eliot started to write in praise of this landscape, and his feeling for it is echoed in *Burnt Norton* and *The Dry Salvages*. It is more than mere local colour; it is an exceptional sense of locality, of the spirit of a place, such as we find also in Faulkner or Julien Green. Claudel's verdict on Supervielle, whom he compared to a mocking-bird whose song has the characteristic of "indicating the place where he is not" might almost be applied to Eliot. He has said that the aim of his poetry or his drama is "to transport the audience violently from one plane of reality to another". There is an element of this in *Burnt Norton* and *The Dry Salvages*.

[31] *After Strange Gods*, 1934, pp. 16, 17. Reprinted in Hayward, op. cit., pp. 216-217.

With *Four Quartets* (1935-1942) we reach, surely, the peak of his lyrical, spiritual work. For since then he seems to have devoted himself above all to dramatic poems, and to essays in Christian and social philosophy.

In 1933, Eliot gave the Page-Barbour Lectures at the University of Virginia, which were afterwards published as *After Strange Gods*; but later, dissatisfied with the tone of the opinions expressed in the work, he opposed its reprinting. Since then, he has concentrated on social problems, on the future development of culture or religion. Such questions form the subject of important studies such as *The Idea of a Christian Society* and *Notes towards a Definition of Culture.* With a keen sense of tradition and of the hierarchy of values, Eliot here seeks to define his attitude towards the Christian community, man and his environment, modern education, the relations between Church and State, the cultural situation, social reform, and the decline of civilization.

The Second World War, from 1939 to 1945, was in many ways a difficult time for Eliot, but it also provided him with an opportunity to demonstrate his devotion to the common cause in a London threatened by enemy air raids. The Blitz, as is well known, inspired a striking passage in the *Quartets*: the description of sunrise ("the uncertain hour before the morning") after the last bomber has gone, in *Little Gidding*.

* *

Three times a week, for forty years, Eliot has gone to his publishers' office in Russell Square, in that part of Bloomsbury which Thackeray used as the setting for his descriptions of the University, but which is now, above all, centred in the British Museum and the University, a meeting-place of intellectuals. In his office on the top floor, Eliot has been a director of the firm Faber and Faber, which has discovered so many young writers and has established so many reputations. Beside a drawing by Wyndham Lewis and a portrait of Valéry, on the walls of a discreetly furnished room, hang reproductions of the works of art that Eliot prizes most highly: the Tomb of Theodoric at Ravenna, St. Zeno at Verona and the Madonna from the large Byzantine mosaic at Murano. No gulf exists between Eliot's style and his life. He has done more than create a new climate of thought; each of his poems marks an entirely new orientation. What he says of Dante is equally applicable to himself: that the poet's intention is less to persuade his readers of the truth of the Christian cosmogony than to make them feel that cosmogony as a personal experience. Whereas talented writers are the interpreters of their age, poets of genius impose their own vision upon their time and mould its style. When in 1934, at the request of an Anglican bishop,[32] Eliot wrote *The Rock,* and then in 1935, at the instance of the Friends of Canterbury, *Murder in the Cathedral,* he did not imagine that his plays would be talked about afterwards. But in fact they were the source of a revival of verse drama in England and the United States: *Murder in the Cathedral* received as much praise in New York as in London, Zurich and Paris. And the same applies to *The Cocktail Party* in 1950.

* *

Confronted with the tribulations of Europe, this devotee of "pure poetry" was moved to meditate on the imminence of various political and social problems, and on the role of culture in a future society. He suspended publication of the *Criterion,* which he had edited for seventeen years.[33] He writes: "In starting the Criterion, I had the aim of bringing together the best new thinking and new writing in its time . . . In the present state of public affairs I no longer feel the enthusiasm necessary to make a literary review what it should be."[34]

* *

[32] George Bell, Bishop of Chichester.

[33] In January 1957 Eliot, a widower for over ten years, married his secretary, Miss Valerie Fletcher.

[34] *Selected Prose,* p. 228.

Since the end of the Second World War, Eliot has received the attention of lovers of literature throughout the world. In 1948 he was awarded the Nobel Prize for Literature, and also the Order of Merit, of which there are only twenty-four holders. He has been heaped with honours: to list them all would be wearisome. Yet he has always remained the same: unaffected, unassuming, courteous and kindly. A growing detachment, an ever-increasing authority, and a strict austerity lend to Eliot's last poems that ascetic charm that Pater describes. No other contemporary poet has such widespread influence: Montale in Italy and many young poets in France bear witness to this, and Auden, Spender or Gascoyne would not wish to dispute it. Not only has Eliot modified the language of poetry by forging a new idiom and laying down a norm of critical requirements; he has also created a movement; he is translated in France, Italy and Germany, and as far afield as India; his plays are performed in Edinburgh, New York and Zurich; Hindus and Estonians annotate his verse. The prodigal son has become a prophet in his own country; there is an Eliot House in Boston, while at Harvard he is the subject of theses. He has been crowned by Sweden and honoured by the Vatican. in 1958, Eliot received a Doctorate, *honoris causa,* at the University of Rome; and to stress his attachment to Latin culture, he delivered his speech of thanks in French. It expressed his debt of gratitude to Virgil and Dante, whom he considers the most human and universal of poets; for he unhesitatingly prefers the Thomist philosophy and the medieval wisdom that inspired Dante to the Renaissance humanism in which Shakespeare is steeped.

How, we may well wonder, did the young American who arrived in London scarcely thirty years before, and whose poetic output can hardly be called voluminous, come to achieve such prestige or such influence? Possibly part of his success is due to the almost prophetic gifts by which he gave us, in his early poems, what Day Lewis has called the image of a society in decay. His vision is penetrating, and he has forged a fit instrument to convey the substance of what he has observed. Between style and substance there is concord, unity and continuity; he has brought a profound intelligence and an intense sensitivity into harmony; and, by precept and example, he has emphasized the mutual dependency of the critical and creative faculties. In a sphere in which nearly all his predecessors pursued only the vapid or the picturesque, or facile charm, he has restored a sense of nobility and seriousness.

2. *The Early Poems*

From Prufrock *to* Gerontion *(1910-1920)*

WHILE VALÉRY'S purpose was "to create a poetic language distinct from ordinary language, as different from practical speech as are the artificial languages of algebra or chemistry", Eliot, on the other hand, seems in his early poems to have tried to capture the tone of everyday speech, the liveliness of phrases used in actual conversation. This does not mean that the form of his verse is any less complex; as he says, he modelled himself on Laforgue's *vers libre* and the highly flexible metre of the later Elizabethan dramatists. He was, in addition, constantly aware of the example of Dante, who also drew on the idiomatic speech of the lower-class women of Florence. Thus in his very sympathy for common idioms he proves to be the heir of the masters of the past, for he believes that the creative act is in great part deliberate and voluntary. His work is basically "consubstantial" with its author; he dislikes its division into various phases. It can best be considered as an indivisible whole, as he himself describes Shakespeare's work: "the whole of Shakespeare is *one* poem . . . united by one significant consistent and developing personality." Though we must resign ourselves here to considering separately the poet, the dramatist, the aesthetician and the sociologist, we shall do our best not to be confined too rigidly by these classifications. "The experience of a poem," Eliot tells us, "is the experience of both a moment and of a lifetime. It is very much like our intenser experiences of other human beings. There is a first or an early moment of shock and surprise, even of terror *(Ego Dominus tuus)*; a moment which can never be forgotten, but which is never repeated integrally, and yet which would become destitute of significance if it did not survive in a larger whole of experience; which survives in a deeper and calmer feeling."[1]

Eliot's poetry has its origins in the intimate, personal experience of an existence "at grips with time and place, torn between the highest spiritual vocation and the most trivial reality, obsessed by a self-abnegation impossible to achieve and by a self-concentration impossible to sustain; constantly jarred and shattered by the invading universe of our civilization".[2]

The idea of experience implies that of progress and renewal. Eliot writes: "A man who is capable of experience finds himself in a different world in every decade of his life; as he sees with different eyes, the material of his art is constantly renewed."[3] With Eliot, however, the transitions are not as abrupt or marked as with certain other poets; the process involved is not one of retrogression, but rather of deepening perception—a continuous, as it were spiral ascent.

Eliot's poetic output can be divided into five distinct periods. To the first belong his youthful verses: *Prufrock and Other Observations* (1917), *Ara Vos Prec*[4] and the *Poems* of 1919, which show the influence of Laforgue and Corbière. The second phase, that of his maturity, is more metaphysical, comprising *Gerontion, The Waste Land* (1922) and *The Hollow Men* (1925). In his third phase, after experiencing agonies of doubt and aridity, the poet gains the sanctuary of the spiritual life and, through it, reconciliation. *The Journey of the Magi* (1927), *A Song for Simeon* (1929), *Animula* (1929), *Marina* (1930), and above all *Ash Wednesday* (1930) join to their religious theme a poignant regret for the earthly affections which the poet has, almost unwillingly, rejected. His *Unfinished Poems* (published at the same time as those of his second and third

[1] From "Dante", (1929). *Selected Prose*, p. 48.

[2] cf. G. A. Astre, "T. S. Eliot, poète spirituel", in *Critique*, April-May 1948.

[3] Yeats Memorial Lecture, reprinted Hayward, op. cit., p. 203.

[4] Title taken from the Provençal verse of Arnaut Daniel, quoted by Dante in the *Inferno*. This collection includes five poems of unequal merit, written in French.

periods) fit into none of these categories: the *Fragment of a Prologue* and *Fragment of an Agon,* and the *Triumphal March* and *Difficulties of a Statesman* are, so to speak, the *disjecta membra* of *Sweeney Agonistes* (1926). And we must not omit the whimsical sketches of *Old Possum's Book of Practical Cats* (1938).

After this, having broached the field of drama and above all having revisited his native land and come to a full awareness of his faith, Eliot wrote between 1935 and 1944 poems which mark the second apogee of his lyrical achievement. On his return to the United States, he felt the stirrings of ancestral sympathies, and mingled private themes with memories of his past, which inspired (besides his play *The Family Reunion*) the *Four Quartets—Burnt Norton, East Coker, The Dry Salvages* and *Little Gidding*. While in *East Coker* the poet returns to his place of origin, *Little Gidding,* in the depths of a winter whiteness which is also spring ("Midwinter spring is its own season") leads the reconciled believer to the sanctuary near Cambridge where Charles I prayed before his death, and where, in troubled times, Nicholas Farrer and the Anglican ritualists kept alive the liturgical traditions of the Church of England.

* *

Let us now trace the course of Eliot's development from the *Preludes* (written about 1910, in Harvard or Paris) through the French poems and *Gerontion* up to *The Waste Land* (written at Lausanne in 1920 and published in 1922). In *The Love Song of J. Alfred Prufrock* (written in Paris and Munich, 1911) Eliot affected a certain "dandyism", relishing his isolation. He emphasized the contrast between the artificial world portrayed by literary men and the trivial details of real life. The middle class that he described was even more bored than that satirized by Corbière and Laforgue. Prufrock at first sees himself surrounded by nothing but "lusts and luxuries", sloth and meanness. The sordidness of everyday life in a large town sickens him; the fetid air, the smoke and fog and mud, the "faint stale smells of beer", the "damp souls of housemaids Sprouting despondently at area gates."

From 1915 to 1920 Eliot sharpened his satiric vein. His poems are like genuine miniature comedies, peopled by incisively-drawn puppets. There is Princess Volupine, symbol of decadent and faded Venice, with her 'meagre, blue-nailed, phthisic hand"; there is "Burbank with a Baedeker", "meditating on Time's ruins, and the Seven Laws"; there is Grishkin whose "friendly bust Gives promise of pneumatic bliss"; above all there is "Apeneck Sweeney", racked by the desires of the flesh, who is a familiar figure in Eliot's later work. Matthiessen has said that Eliot first glimpsed the prototype of Sweeney in a bar in South Boston. Here the character springs to life in a vivid, almost hallucinatory way; Eliot recognizes an element of his own personality in the repulsive stranger, and has therefore got inside him and endowed him with his own feelings and opinions. Eliot has thus created living characters from his interpretation and analysis of his own emotions and experience. One such figure is J. Alfred Prufrock, the fictional author of the early poems, where we already come across the themes and images which recur in the later works. Matthiessen writes: "Eliot was fascinated by the way in which James did not simply relate but made the reader co-operate . . . by the way, for example, in *The Aspern Papers* he managed to give the whole feeling of Venice by the most economical strokes. Indeed, Eliot has recently said that the method in this story—*to make a place real not descriptively but by something happening there*—was what stimulated him to compress so many memories of past moments of Venice into his dramatic poem."[5] Like Proust, Eliot has the gift of *rediscovering* certain rare places, where time is embodied in space—the gift not merely of "reviving" the moments of the vanished past, but of making us aware of time's passage while immortalizing certain timeless presences.

More than any other contemporary poet, Eliot is sensitive to that "pressure of the past upon the present", to the climate

[5] F. O. Matthiessen, *The Achievement of T. S. Eliot,* New York.

and rhythm of the period. He is also concerned with what he calls "the pattern", which can be compared to Hopkins' "inscape". All Eliot's work aims at bridging the gulf which yawns between poetry and the modern world. Admittedly the poetry of the French Symbolists led to the experiments of such writers as Apollinaire and Max Jacob, as well as to those of Eliot. But the author of *Prufrock* did not wait for Cubism or Futurism to celebrate the new look of the world; in contrast to the Surrealists, Eliot combines a concern for order with a yearning for dream, and for the turbulence of ecstasy; he has not sought to break open the doors of the world beyond, nor to reveal the innermost secret of things. He did not believe that automatic writing would eventually supersede logical expression. And his liking for the barbaric did not mean that he undervalued the Classics. He was aware that, in Mallarmé's phrase, "there is nothing in the world that cannot be expressed by the ancient and sacred art of words". Thus every poem of Eliot's is an enigma, creating "a new word, foreign to the language and as it were incantatory." Knowing that music and literature are "the two faces of a single phenomenon, the *Idea*", Eliot, "with instinctive rhythms", controls "the form and movement of each consonant". His poetry is "music without the tumult of sonorities". (Mallarmé)

Eliot reintroduced abstract thought into poetry, and combined it with the "immediate emotions" which the poet "provokes". As Pater advised, he achieved the perfection of pure poetry by suppressing all that was not the subject, so that the meaning of the poem is conveyed to us by ways unfamiliar to the understanding. As Eliot tells us, the poem is dictated not by the idea but by the nature of that dark embryo within the poet which gradually assumes the form and language of the poem.[6] "The poet has, not a 'personality' to express, but a particular medium, which is only a medium and not a personality, in which impressions and experiences combine in peculiar and unexpected ways."[7]

[6] Introduction to the Poems of Harold Monro.
[7] *The Sacred Wood,* p. 53.

Eliot has the gift of vividly evoking a particular landscape, scene or place; in a few lines he conjures up an image of a foggy morning in an Oxford or Boston street:

"They are rattling breakfast plates in basement kitchens
And along the trampled edges of the street
I am aware of the damp souls of housemaids
Sprouting despondently at area gates.[8]
The brown waves of fog toss up to me
Twisted faces from the bottom of the street,
And tear from a passer-by with muddy skirts
An aimless smile that hovers in the air
And vanishes along the level of the roofs."[9]

* *

So perfect a prosody is not achieved overnight. The language, the rhythm, the metre—each has its antecedents. Through centuries of use, through the way it was handled by Wordsworth and Browning, and above all by Donne, Marvell, Crashaw and other "metaphysical" (distinguished by Eliot from "philosophical") poets, English verse now seems suited to the rendering of abstract speculation without becoming prosaic, or rather, while bordering on prose, never actually descending to the commonplace. Eliot derives his skill as much from such predecessors as from Laforgue, Corbière and Ezra Pound (the *miglior fabbro* to whom *The Waste Land* is dedicated). He tells us that he found in the French Symbolists, as in the early seventeenth-century English poets and dramatists, "the same essential quality of transmuting ideas into sensations, of transforming an observation into a state of mind" (*The Metaphysical Poets*). By combining disparate images, Eliot's verse does indeed "surprise by a fine excess", to use Keat's words. It was from Baudelaire, above all, that he learned to extend the whole range of poetry by drawing on images from the daily life of a great metropolis,

[8] cf. Flaubert: "When I was quite young, I was already fully aware of what life would be like. It was like a sickening kitchen-smell rising up from a grating." (*Correspondence,* I, 201).

[9] *Prufrock and Other Observations*: Morning at the Window.

with the squalid labyrinth of its working-class districts, its rag-and-bone men and its dingy suburbs. Baudelaire went further: he achieved "the elevation of such imagery to the first intensity, presenting it as it is and yet making it represent something much more than itself" (Eliot). Baudelaire was, in the nineteenth century, as Racine was in the seventeenth, supreme in his mastery of diction and in his psychological penetration. Even his "satanism" goes beyond Romantic blasphemy, or Huysmans' erudite and picturesque realism; it is genuinely concerned with the Fall and the Redemption, with "softening the effects of Original Sin". And it is this which, in a hypocritical world, distinguishes Baudelaire's faith from the "modernist Protestantism of Byron and Shelley."

> "Baudelaire is indeed the greatest exemplar in *modern* poetry in any language, for his verse and language is the nearest thing to a complete renovation that we have experienced. But his renovation of an attitude towards life is no less radical and no less important. In his verse he is now less a model to be imitated or a source to be drained than a reminder of the duty, the consecrated task, of sincerity."[10]
>
> "One difference between Baudelaire and the later poets—Laforgue, Verlaine, Corbière, Rimbaud, Mallarmé—is that Baudelaire not only reveals the troubles of his own age and predicts those of the age to come, but also foreshadows some issue from these difficulties. When we get to Laforgue, we find a poet who seems to express more clearly even than Baudelaire the difficulties of his own age; he speaks to us, or spoke to my generation, more intimately than Baudelaire seemed to do. Only later we conclude that Laforgue's "present" is a narrower present than Baudelaire's, and that Baudelaire's present extends to more of the past and more of the future."[11]

Eliot admits nevertheless that his passion for Laforgue possessed him like a spell cast by a more powerful personality.[12]

[10] Preface to Baudelaire's *Journaux Intimes,* in *Selected Essays* (1958) p. 426.

[11] Review of Peter Quennell's *Baudelaire and the Symbolists, The Criterion,* January 1930, pp. 357-8.

[12] Letter to Mr E. Greene, October 18th 1939.

Yet the disciple was already far more assured than his master, that poor "Lord Pierrot", "imprisoned in his own adolescence" ! Eliot has observed that Donne, Corbière and Laforgue "begin with their own feelings, and their limitation is that they do not always get much outside or beyond; Shakespeare, one feels, arrives at an objective world by a process from himself, whoever he was, as the centre and starting-point; but too often one thinks with Browning, here is a world with no particular interesting man in it, no consistent point of view. But the verse method in all these four men is similar; either dramatic monologue or dramatic dialogue; and with Donne and the French poets, the pattern is given by what goes on within the mind, rather than by the exterior events which provoke the mental activity and play of thoughts and feeling."[13]

The hold which Baudelaire, Corbière and Laforgue exerted over Eliot is the equivalent of the influence which French painting had (and still has) on English and American painters. Manet, Seurat and Toulouse-Lautrec revealed to them—apart from matters of technique, form and texture—that there are no "noble subjects" in art; that the meanest object, the humblest tool, can be given grandeur in painting; that in the trivial details of modern life, even in machines themselves, may be found as much poetry and beauty as in the most treasured antique jewellery. In contrast to many writers who are disillusioned or indifferent, Eliot is appalled by the savagery of life. We feel that like Dostoievsky he is obsessed by "the outrage done to the little girl." Thus his poetry is made up of "velleities and carefully caught regrets" . . .[14] Above all, it has the same bitter irony that we find in Laforgue's *Derniers Vers.* Such

[13] *A Garland for John Donne,* pp. 75-76.

[14] How does this poetry, with its copious borrowings, retain such an intensely personal accent and tone? Doubtless, as Stephen Spender has suggested, "the seriousness of Eliot's earlier poetry is conveyed by the impression it forces that there is indeed only one problem: is the soul of the individual capable of being saved, damned, or in any way morally judged?" *The Destructive Element,* Jonathan Cape, London, 1935, p. 139.

poetry is first and foremost *psychology*. Sometimes, too, we hear echoes of Verlaine—"poor Lélian's" *ariettes:*

> *"C'est la ville où se caille et se lie*
> *Ce passé qu'on boit jusqu'a la lie . . ."*[15]

Precision of style is reached through the use of metaphor (or, as the English called it in the seventeenth century, the conceit). It has been said (by T. E. Hulme) that metaphor is functional, not ornamental; it enables us to learn the state of mind of the poet at work. It is an image in which the act of imagination has itself become analytical; and the extended metaphor is successful in proportion as idea and figure are one, while the condensed metaphor is successful when the image is the very embodiment of the thought. Hulme comments that poetry is sincere when the entire analogy is necessary in order to obtain the exact curve of the emotion or the object that you wish to express . . .

> "The only way of expressing emotion in the form of art is by finding an 'objective correlative'; in other words, a set of objects, a situation, a chain of events which shall be the formula of that *particular* emotion; such that when the external facts, which must terminate in sensory experience, are given, the emotion is immediately evoked." (*The Sacred Wood,* p. 100).

This view, we may observe, is akin to Proust's "sensation-memory", by which we suddenly re-experience the emotion we formerly felt, as if our past were recaptured in the object or event incorporating it by *the transformation of memory into directly experienced reality*. Eliot, no doubt, thinks like Proust that we can "find beauty in a rubber tyre or a piece of stuff as much as in a mountain or in the sky." And the author of *Four Quartets* would not contradict the author of *Le Temps Retrouvé* when he asserts that our life, "dissatisfied with the present, saddened by the past, is designed to enjoy eternity." Both writers have sought, in places and at times of special sig-

[15] Verlaine, *Arieltes oubliées.*

nificance, "that timeless moment when time no longer conceals what is essential."[16]

Like many American writers, Eliot feels, confronted with the modern world, a twofold disquiet: estrangement and frustration. He knows that the poet has a duty to be the interpreter of his age; on the other hand he is sickened by the futility and ugliness of contemporary life; and this is the reason for the irony and sardonic jesting of his early poems. Yet Prufrock admits, like Nerval, that he has "heard the mermaids singing, each to each . . ." adding, however,

> "I do not think that they will sing to me.
> I have seen them riding seaward on the waves
> Combing the white hair of the sea blown back
> When the wind blows the water white and black
>
> We have lingered in the chambers of the sea
> By sea-girls wreathed with seaweed red and brown
> Till human voices wake us, and we drown."

Eliot has been attracted by many French poets; the influences vary in intensity, kind or duration. Baudelaire's influence seems to have been the strongest and most persistent; together with that of Dante and Pascal it has affected not only his poetry but also his critical thought, both religious and social. Laforgue and Corbière were only the masters he followed in his youth; while about 1920 he took as model, from a purely formal point of view, the highly elaborate verse of Théophile Gautier and Laurent Tailhade. Lastly, his debt to St John Perse and Stéphane Mallarmé can be felt in the poems of his maturity. According to Eliot, Laforgue was, if not the greatest French poet since Baudelaire, at any rate the most important technical innovator:

> "The *vers libre* of Jules Laforgue . . . is free verse in much the way that the later verse of Shakespeare, Webster, Tourneur is free verse; that is to say, it stretches, contracts and distorts the traditional French measure as later Elizabethan and Jaco-

[16] Marcel Proust, *Le Temps Retrouvé, II,* 15-18.

bean poetry stretches, contracts and distorts the blank verse measure. But the term is applied to several types of verse which have developed in English without relation to Laforgue, Corbière and Rimbaud or to each other. To be precise, there are for instance my own type of verse, that of Pound, and that of the disciples of Whitman. I will not say that subsequently there have not appeared traces of reciprocal influence of several types upon one another, but I am here speaking of origins. My own verse is, so far as I can judge, nearer to the original meaning of *vers libre* than is any of the other types."[17]

Our era, Eliot declares, is hostile to the sublime and cannot tolerate the simplification or separation of mental faculties. Whatever our opinion on this point may be, Eliot has undeniably given expression to one of the modes of feeling of the first half of the twentieth century. Identifying the Universe with its Idea, he "fills the metaphysical form with a content of familiar, concrete and definite impressions". The *lampion forain,* the street-fair lantern to which Laforgue compared his heart, the "dying yellow gaslight of the misty boulevards" became the spluttering street-lamp in the yellow Thames-side fog. Eliot inherited also from Laforgue his fondness for "pale lilacs", for the "drowned heart", for broom and cactus and for many an abstract term . . . As for Mallarmé, Eliot carries on his entire aesthetic system of allusiveness (and elusiveness): those "condensed glories", the "demon of analogy", the "interrelatedness of everything", an obsession with certain recurrent images such as that of hair.[18] It is true that Poe was the first to prove that "no point in a composition can be attributed to chance or intuition" and that a work of art proceeds step by step towards its solution with the precise and strict logic of a mathematical problem. But it is Baudelaire alone who shows us how to link

[17] Introduction to *Selected Poems by Ezra Pound,* p. viii.

[18] See the remarkable first chapter of E. J. H. Greene's *T. S. Eliot et la France,* to which I am indebted for more than one reference. Mr Green questions my suggestion of a possible influence by Lautréamont on Eliot, since the poet himself denies any awareness of such influence. Eliot might have seen fragments of *Maldoror* which appeared in *The Egoist,* October 1914, and might unconsciously have caught certain echoes of Ducasse's poetry through St-John Perse and Laforgue.

sensation and intellect while excluding sentiment, Baudelaire who teaches us to seek everywhere the fleeting beauty of the present moment *(la beauté passagère, fugace, de la vie présente)*, and it was from Baudelaire that Eliot learnt personification, giving abstract ideas bodily substance. Finally, Baudelaire foreshadowed Eliot's Christianity by reacting against the Hegelian idealism and the logomachy of his time. Both of them hate *"le vague à l'âme"*, vague spirituality, no less than the spontaneous and impulsive. Both transform their discontent into a *principle of conquest* and, by the tension of their over-alert nerves, give to their allegories a "veiled density". They have much in common: the lure of the sea, an obsession with the city and its suburbs, "spleen" and *angst,* remorse and irony, even a lot of cats—*les chats puissants et doux*—whose acid mewings they mimic.[19] Peter Quennell has compared Eliot's rhetoric to the art of Baudelaire, as defined by Laforgue:

> "Mr Eliot has emulated a characteristic of Baudelaire's poetic method which Laforgue called his 'Yankeeism', his tautness, that is to say the abrupt, unnatural cast of his sentences, his habit of deliberately interposing some startling, bathetic piece of imagery . . ."[20]

This rhetoric finds an admirable vehicle in Eliot's unrhymed verse, whose secret he has thus described:

> "When the comforting echo of rhyme is removed, success or failure in the choice of words, in the sentence structure, in the order, is at once more apparent . . . And this liberation from rhyme might be as well a liberation *of* rhyme. Freed from its exacting task of supporting lame verse, it could be applied with greater effect where it is most needed."[21]

Although his verse has the spontaneous tone of conversation, it is also algebra and music; it is a secret language, a cipher, a ritual dance, a magic spell. The intellect, the sense and the heart together give a persuasive, obsessive force to his words.

[19] *Old Possum's Book of Practical Cats.*
[20] *Life and Letters,* March 1929.
[21] *New Statesman,* March 3rd 1917.

Baudelaire showed that "rhythm and rhyme fulfil man's immortal need for monotony, symmetry and surprise". Like his master, Eliot mistrusts "the vanity and danger of inspiration". He knows how "poetry borders on music, by way of a prosody whose roots go deeper into the human soul than any Classical theory indicates". The words are less important than the tone. Eliot has, as Scarfe puts it, "renounced poetry in order to regain it". Of his early poems it might be said (to paraphrase Baudelaire's words) that "everything in them is both head and tail, alternately and reciprocally". Baudelaire, inspired by Aloysius Bertrand, had the idea of "applying to the description of modern life, or rather of a particular more abstract modern life" the method which the author of *Gaspard de la Nuit* had used for describing the life of former times. Eliot did not resort to prose, as they had done; he created a kind of verse very close to ordinary speech, and a system of prosody "sufficiently supple and irregular to fit the lyrical movements of the soul, the undulations of reverie and the fits and starts of consciousness". "It was chiefly from dwelling in huge cities," (London, Paris, New York) "it was from the network of their complex associations that this obsessive ideal arose." Perhaps Baudelaire was the precursor of *The Waste Land* when he describes a town as

> *"Un désert rocailleux troublé par des cris aigres"*
> (A rocky desert, disturbed by shrill cries)

Sometimes the poet's tensed nerves produce "plangent and sorrowful vibrations". At all events, the poet of *Les Fleurs du Mal* (and friend of Meryon, the Englishman who painted Paris) revealed the *"charme infernal"*, the infernal attraction of the city, seen in all its breadth :

> *"Hôpital, lupanar, purgatoire, enfer, bagne"*
> (Hospital, brothel, purgatory, hell, prison)

Surely it was from Baudelaire that Eliot derived his vision of that "vast dusty plain, pathless, grassless, where no thistle or nettle will grow", that "stagnant atmosphere" haunted by the "somnambulic life" of the mineral world. It was Baudelaire who revealed to him the "sour smell of desolation," the "nauseating reek of decay" in a "mean world, sick at heart" surrounded by the *meubles sots,* the futile trimmings and trivialities of life. He experienced hatred of merciless Time, with its "demon train of memories, regrets, spasms, terrors, anguish and nightmare . . ." He "climbed the mysterious stairway by which the forces of hell assault defenceless, sleeping man and hold secret communication with him". Eliot has observed, perhaps with Nerval in mind as much as Dante, that we have lost the habit of disciplining our dreams.

Finally, how could he fail to be attracted by the intimate, elliptic lyricism of Corbière—that new barbaric Villon with the harsh, strangled voice.

> *"Cri, d'os, dur, sec, qui plaque et casse—plangorer?"*[22]
> (The cry of a hard dry bone snapping—a lamentation?)

How could he fail to recognize an elder brother in that "contumacious poet", that "untamed animal", that "long, lean, pallid layabout", that "amateur hermit" of whom the Bretons said: "He must be an Englishman" . . . Was not Eliot himself a

> *"jeune philosophe en dérive*
> *Revenu sans avoir été?"*[23]
>
> (Young philosopher adrift. Back again from where he had never been).

As a disciple of this cross-grained, melancholy, eccentric rhymer, whose language was full of dipthongs and diaereses, the promising American poet was so enthralled by the strange charm of this queer, unhealthy genius that he borrowed the tone of his "lunar rhapsodies", his "fairground songs", his "broken idylls" where impudent banter mingles with bitter pathos. He borrowed, too, for a while—deserting his own language—not only the "blasphemies, pirouettes and genuflexions", the nonsense verse, the crazy conceits (in which, to quote Huysmans, there suddenly breaks out a scream of pain as shrill as a snapping 'cello string), not only that abrupt, ungainly prosody, harsh,

[22] *Les Amours Jaunes.* [23] ibid.

broken, disconnected; not only that deliberate awkwardness, those jerky movements, the artful naïvety as of a deaf bard playing an out-of-tune barrel organ, but something more; Eliot was to follow Corbière into that somnambulist's slumber, into that

> *"pays où le muet se réveille prophète"*
> (country where the deaf man awakes to find himself a prophet)

And adopting as his own Corbière's Brittany, Eliot absorbed—from that "poverty-stricken rocky land, unfriendly and tattered", that land of joy and mystery which is nothing but "dust of dead bones," where "the rosy grass is verminous"—the setting for his own *Waste Land* and *Hollow Men*. Henceforward, like that "morbid poet of darkness" *(cet hystérique du ténébreux)* he began quite naturally to pose, deluding himself with witticisms, mimicking the epitaph of the "cynical master-philosopher"; like Corbière, studding his verse with foreign words, titles, fragments and refrains from every language he knew, and even adopting as his motto the words inscribed by Corbière below his epitaph concerning the things "in whose beginning is their end" . . .

Prufrock, however, already has a more arresting and powerful tone than the *Moralités Légendaires* or the *Amours Jaunes*. We are far from the shrill plaintiveness of the one, the bitter irony and self-pitying sobs of the other; far from the decadent play-acting of the two *"poètes maudits"* . . . For Eliot makes use of the glamour of the past to adorn the grim gloom of the present, giving contemporary life the resonance of the enduring. Although he had as yet nothing of the mystic about him, Eliot had already learnt self-enrichment through self-deprivation. By borrowing from others, he had acquired an inimitable personality. Besides, as Chateaubriand said, the great writer is not he who imitates nobody, but he whom nobody is able to imitate.

* *

Eliot's poems in French, it must be observed, are in a particularly sardonic vein, and seem to lack the essential charm of his English verse. Only the end of the poem *Dans le Restaurant* seems worthy of the author of *Prufrock* and *Sweeney*; in it we come across some of his future themes and even the accent of the great later poems, from *The Waste Land* to *Marina*:

"Phlébas le Phenicien, pendant quinze jours noyé,
Oubliait les cris des mouettes et la houle de Cornouailles
Et les profits et les pertes et la cargaison d'étain . . ."
(This passage recurs in *The Waste Land*.)

It was about 1920 that T. S. Eliot and Ezra Pound,[24] in reaction against the over-facility of *vers librisme*, of free verse according to Amy Lowell and Edgar Lee Masters, decided to return to the strictest form, the most clear-cut verse of all: the octosyllabic line as used by Théophile Gautier in his *Emaux et Camées*. But for mature poets such as Eliot and Pound this was more than an exercise in prosody, a sort of metrical discipline. We can see how Eliot transforms a purely picturesque poem of Gautier's, *"L'Hippopotame"*, into a mock-solemn chant rich in ironical and humorous implications. Lastly, in *Sweeney among the Nightingales,* the tone is insensibly heightened, so much as that the last strophe (as Yeats observed) reminds us irresistably of Classical poetry:

"The host with someone indistinct
Converses at the door apart,
The nightingales are singing near
The Convent of the Sacred Heart,

And sang within the bloody wood
When Agamemnon cried aloud,
And let their liquid siftings fall
To stain the stiff dishonoured shroud."[25]

* *

[24] About the same time they were attracted by the doctrines of Charles Maurras.

[25] *Sweeney Among the Nightingales, Poems,* 1920.

The whole of Eliot's first phase might well bear as inscription de Gourmont's epigram on Flaubert: "The only real books are those in which an author describes himself while describing the ways of his contemporaries—their dreams, their vanity, their love affairs and their foolish acts." Each of these short poems contains a potential drama, and a complete character is conveyed by the slightest stroke—or rather is set before us, both potentially and actually. What concerns the poet is human experiences, important not because they are his own but in themselves, in their own right. This does not prevent him from sincerely trying to educe general laws from his personal impressions. Instead of writing subjective, emotional poems, as the Romantics did, Eliot, like Flaubert, chose to take symbolic types as his protagonists, to "incorporate" in them "his whole sensibility" (occasionally even his weaknesses and obsessions) and to "pour himself into them drop by drop".

Some critics rank Eliot's youthful poems above those of his maturity. One cannot but admire their caustic wit and their restrained irony. One of Eliot's poetic methods, as pointed out by Allen Tate,[26] is to project *simultaneously* events which are separate in duration destroying the perception of the usual categories of time and space and giving the illusion of chaos.

From 1919 onwards Eliot was constantly concerned with contrasting the vulgarity of the present with the splendour of the past—a contrast which was to form one of the themes of *The Waste Land*. In every poem, from *Sweeney* to *Gerontion* (as, later on, from *The Magi* to *Simeon*), underlying the allegory or parable it presents, there is an ulterior motive: "to redeem the time and the dream."

Like his own Gerontion, Eliot stands before us

> "   in a dry month,
> Being read to by a boy, waiting for rain."

Then presently "came Christ the tiger," who devoured him.

[26] A Poetry of Ideas, New Republic, June 30th 1926, p. 172.

3. *From* The Waste Land *to* Marina

IN HIS great poem *The Waste Land,* Eliot speaks to us for the first time in that harsh, grave, rather dry voice that, once heard, is unforgettable; the curt, abrupt rhythms, the muted, desolate intonation of a deeply secret soul. The poet here speaks for a shipwrecked world; about to sink, he sees in a flash, as drowning men do, the whole of his past. But this poem is not only a "song of remembrance"; it is the expression of a longing for order. Eliot uses metaphysical doctrines in order to sharpen and strengthen his visual and emotional powers. His work involves a broadening of his own sensibility, the discovery of new objects that will awaken new emotions. The real world is enlarged by him. And he moves with a firm step from the tangible world into the world of ghosts.[1]

Eliot here provides "the impression of a life that is more intense and yet more fluid, more ephemeral than real life." We breathe "that centuries-old exhalation, narcotic and funereal as the odour of a mummy", in Flaubert's phrase.[2] Like Joyce in *Ulysses,* Eliot constantly emphasizes the parallels between contemporary events and the myths of antiquity. He is, moreover, aware of the resemblance between his own work and that of Joyce. A creative artist often chooses to follow an outline already laid down, pouring the substance of his personal genius into a ready-made mould, especially as the themes of pagan mythology are rich in esoteric meanings which convey

[1] cf. T. S. Eliot, *Poe et Mallarmé,* N.R.F.

[2] Flaubert, *L'Education Sentimentale,* pp. 461-463 and *La Spirale.*

to us the symbols of primitive humanity or the wisdom of ages. As much through reading as through experience of life, certain memories become loaded with a weight of authoritative emotions.

Eliot considers that the historical sense is "nearly indispensible to anyone who would continue to be a poet beyond his twenty-fifth year"; and that is precisely "what makes a writer most acutely conscious of his place in time, of his own contemporaneity". Through his own private sorrows and ecstasies, it has been emphasized, Eliot "grasps the secret meaning of his age. In reality the 'I' of his poems does not express the 'feeling self'; it is rather the protagonist of a tragic or satiric chorus." In this way Eliot projects "into symbolic figures those feelings which in the more fluid form or direct, purely lyrical confession could not acquire complete historic significance but would lapse into didacticism."[3]

Eliot asserts that: "Our civilization comprehends great variety and complexity, and this variety and complexity, playing upon a refined sensibility, must produce various and complex results. The poet must become more and more complex, more allusive, more indirect, in order to force, to dislocate if necessary, language into his meaning."[4] His art is based on *ellipsis;* even more than the sense, what matters is the intonation, the rhythm, a syncopated, spasmodic rhythm. In his metaphors the first term is often submerged, the analogy is hidden, hinted at; the transsubstantiation is carried out through the image. Of course Eliot wants to be understood, but like Coleridge he considers that poetry gives the greatest pleasure when it is understood as a whole, and not too distinctly. "Critics sometimes comment" he says "upon the sudden transitions and juxtapositions of modern poetry. Whether the transition is cogent or not is merely a question of whether the mind is *serré* or *délié*, whether the whole personality is involved."[5]

[3] Louis Bolle, *"L'Oeuvre poétique de T. S. Eliot"*, La Gazette de Lausanne, June 5th 1954.

[4] *The Metaphysical Poets.*

[5] *Selected Essays,* p. 462.

And he concludes with words which might be applied to his own poetry:

> ". . . it is the unity of a personality which gives an indissoluable unity to his variety of subject."

Eliot's poetry attempts to marry the magic of incantation with strict observance of the law. He chooses themes rich in echoes and memories. If he despises all cheap verbal and rhetorical effects, the pungency of aphorisms, the pathos of apostrophes, the bite of invective, virtuosity and glitter, he seeks to condense his dreams into dream-figures, to reduce an event to an image, to transform superficial appearances into symbols. For his poetry, "transcendent" like that of Novalis, "deals with spiritual things before they have become spiritual."

For thirty years critics have been commenting on Eliot's verse, but everything has not yet been said. This is not through any lack of fantasy or imagination on the critics' part. Some have interpreted the symbolism of his poetry according to their own lights; others have approached it from the point of view of their own psychological experience, finally there are others who, following Dr Johnson's tradition, have given us more lucid analyses of his work, since they do not attempt to superimpose extraneous ideas on those of the author. In his plays, as in his criticisms, Eliot's approach has always been by way of poetic apprehension. He has, however, always avoided the temptation of making use of language alone as a source of fertilization. Our task here is to pinpoint the reasons for the "obscurity" of which he has often been accused. His poetry is certainly difficult, elliptic and discontinuous, since he combines a remarkable variety of forms. It is not a question, therefore, of distinguishing form and content, but of showing that the esoteric quality of his verse is required by the nature of the age of which he is interpreter; he succeeds in focusing our attention on the object, not on the means of expression. Certain repetitions may give an incantatory effect to his most straightforward utterance, as in *Journey of the Magi;* this is because his auditory imagination assumes an authentic suggestive power. Rivalling Baudelaire in his use of "correspondences", Rimbaud in his "verbal alchemy" and Mallarmé in his "invention of a language", Eliot gives new life to the symbols and idioms borrowed from various realms. New vistas open before us; we experience sensations of extension in time and space which belong only to music; orchestration, counterpoint, fugue, syncopation, consonance and dissonance, harmony, polyphony and rest . . . Certain poems, like Chinese ideograms which juxtapose contrasting images, have been described as "hieroglyphic puzzles" or, as Claudel has said, "a kind of sibylline provocation for Oedipus to interpret." Closer study convinces us that these disparate and disjointed things form a coherent whole.

In *The Waste Land* Eliot was using the method which recurs in most of his recent poems: to contrast two kinds of "life" and two kinds of "death" : a life devoid of significance is in fact a "death", while the act of sacrifice may bring awakening to new life. The poem is a sequence of variations on this theme. Mankind, having lost the sense of Good and Evil, has ceased to be alive. The "waste land" is the region that has been devastated, scorched, laid bare, stricken with sterility, and also the deserted arid no-man's-land, a realm whose inhabitants are sleepwalkers, only half alive. In the Greek text which Eliot quotes as inscription, the Sibyl pronounces: "I want to die". And this seems to be the wish of the ghosts that people the "dead land"; as in the *Journey of the Magi,* they seem to say: "I should be glad of another death." Are they not already half dead, rotting away like the dead trees of the bewitched kingdom described in the old legends of the Round Table? In the *Quest for the Holy Grail* can be found, hidden many layers deep, the last echo of ancient myths and mysteries. The themes of the Grail correspond in striking fashion to Eliot's own conflicts. The whole of his Puritan adolescence had been concerned with death and the desires of the flesh; he had been obsessed by the awareness of sin. From the symbolism of this Breton legend, therefore, as from folk tales of all lands and all ages, he derived the theme of his "apocalypse", purposely interweaving different epochs and different traditions. In the background of the poem we recognize the animistic concept of the Year-God's resurrection. Eliot even draws on the Tarot card pack[6] in which occur, distorted or transposed, the symbols of the Grail (the chalice is represented by "hearts", the spear by "diamonds", the sword by "spades" and the dish by "clubs") and in which appear the Hanged God and the Drowned Man of primitive fertility rites.

Eliot makes no secret of his debt, for the title, theme and symbolism of his poem, to the works of Frazer, Mead and above all Jessie L. Weston.[7] What is most striking about these borrowings is the "receptive poetic spirit" which caught the echo of its own nostalgic longings even in the primitive form of magic symbolism. Following the work of Mannhardt, Harrison and Shöcrder, who revealed the importance of vegetation cults—the death and resurrection of Osiris, Attis, Adonis, symbols of the natural cycles of growth and decay—Jessie Weston showed that the Quest for the Grail can be traced back to very ancient rites later incorporated into the Christian legends. It was a subsequent theory that linked the Grail to the chalice of the Mass, and the hero's spear to that of Longinus. *The Waste Land,* then, was a poem about the shipwreck of civilizations, about the elements and the seasons, about rites and mysteries and trade, and lust, and cosmogonies, and Eastern initiations, and the Tarot pack, and Tradition, and the humblest nonsense songs. It is a poem whose spokesman is the "old man with wrinkled female breasts"—Tiresias, the blind seer, who becomes one with the Phenician sailor and the shipwrecked prince of Shakespeare's *Tempest*! For *The Waste Land* is a mystery play with three characters. The first—and the most important, who epitomizes all the rest, and in whom finally the two sexes meet —is the Fisher King, who is in fact identical with Tiresias—call him Mehaigne or Amfortas as you please. The second figure is Cleopatra, alias Dido, or Queen Elizabeth, or the

[6] Originally the Tarot pack served to foretell not the future, but the rise of fertilizing waters.

[7] Jessie L. Weston, *From Ritual to Romance.* On the source of the Grail myth see the recent work of Jean Marx.

Lithuanian woman, the clairvoyante, the typist who is seduced . . . As for the third character, the champion of the Grail he is no longer Percival of Wales, or Galahad, or Gawain; he is "the Smyrna merchant, unshaven, with a pocket full of currants": Mr Eumenides, who is no other, as we have observed, than Phlebas the Phoenician, Ferdinand Prince of Naples, the Drowned Man of the Tarot pack whom Madame Sosostris, famous clairvoyante, sees in her cards . . .

Eliot's irony undermines the most pompous façades, and the most solemn occasions. Nothing is spared. In order to shed a clearer light on man in his relations with the universe, Eliot portrays him wrestling not only with the basic problems of existence but also with the most trivial difficulties of daily life, since the present is continually interrupted by the intrusion of the past.[8] The themes touched on by Eliot in this "poem which is more than a poem" are based on the concept of the Four Elements, together with Time, which brings about alterations. The five movements develop thus: I. The Burial of the Dead, II. A Game of Chess, III. The Fire Sermon, IV. Death by Water, V. What the Thunder said. In the first canto, *The Burial of the Dead,* as in an overture, a number of themes are started which recur later in the poem. It is April, the season of renewal, of the germination of seed, of the juvescence of the year. But the dwellers in the Waste Land dread such an awakening to life:

> "April is the cruellest month, breeding
> Lilacs out of the dead land, mixing
> Memory and desire, stirring
> Dull roots with spring rain."

This "cruel April" is, it has been noted, the awakening of a new awareness. With the storm, the arid soil stirs with the

[8] In connection with the "broken images" in the opening of *The Waste Land* it has been noted that Rupert Brooke, describing a friend's feelings on learning that war had been declared, enumerates the confused images suggested to his mind by the word "Germany"; many of these resemble those of *The Waste Land,* (See John Finley jr. quoted by F. O. Matthiessen.)

promise of life. The Lost Land will be redeemed, liberated, life and death are no longer contradictions. Everything is confused: present, past and future are simultaneous. (Did not Henry James have a similar sense of the reversibility of time?) Yesterday's hero, who is also today's, can exclaim:

> "And I Tiresias have foresuffered all
> Enacted on this same divan or bed;
> I who have sat by Thebes below the wall
> And walked among the lowest of the dead."

For what blind Tiresias, "throbbing between two lives", *sees* is the very essence of this twilight poem. *The Waste Land* stigmatizes the barren loves of our modern Babylon (which are akin to the "cauldron of unholy loves" of Carthage) and the poet here recalls St Augustine, who witnessed the Barbarian invasion and the collapse of a civilization, the death of a whole world, and yet foresaw the birth of a new world, described the features of the coming age, and "burning, burning, burning"—forged its very spirit. The narrator of the poem, too, is on the eve of some momentous resurrection.

At the end of the first canto, we were among the dead, among those with "lidless eyes" who can do nothing but remember. This desolate land is a frightful limbo (like Sartre's *Huis Clos*), peopled by ghosts, a nightmare blend of death and life, if, one can call these creeping rats alive. For Eliot, long before Sartre, used images of viscosity and nausea . . . Eliot also tends to combine opposites, to transcend paradoxes. *The Waste Land* is based not only on interwoven symbols of drought and rain but also on the frequent recurrence of the theme of the Unreal City. This is the *terra deserta et inaquosa* mentioned in the Scriptures. Ezekiel's stony desert and dry bones were awaiting the water that would bring life; whereas we are given only images of polluted water, the Thames bearing its cardboard boxes and cigarette ends, and the "dull canal" with its reek of dead rats. And the hero dreads death by drowning.

The poet here becomes "the historian of the future". He speaks for the men of tomorrow. He foresees the catastrophe:

"Jerusalem Athens Alexandria
Vienna London
Unreal"

What, then, is the city to which Eliot refers at the end of his first Canto? It is not only the modern metropolis that Baudelaire described:

"Fourmillante cité, cité pleine de rêves
Où le spectre en plein jour raccroche le passant . . ."

This town, drowned in the "brown fog of a winter morning", symbolizes the aimless flux of a post-war multitude, who no longer have any purpose, any faith, or any hope, and who gaze at a heap of broken idols with the same helpless sadness as the shades wandering through Dante's *Limbo,* where are gathered those who on earth have incurred "neither praise nor blame". We are reminded of the vision of Hieronymus Bosch, or those stony wildernesses which the school of Ferrara painted as background to their Biblical scenes. Such as the withered kingdom, the terrifying world in which bourgeois civilization, governed by fear, can no longer remain honourable. Here we behold the essential malaise of the human soul. And that is why this lifeless humanity is represented now in the person of Osiris, Adonis, or Orpheus, and now in the person of Christ himself.

Eliot gives meaning to the "immense panorama of anarchy and futility presented by contemporary history". It is not that he had abandoned all hope; replying to those who saw in his work only the reflection of their own nihilism, he wrote: "I may have expressed for them their own illusion of being disillusioned, but that did not form part of my intention."[9] Far from expressing absolute despair, Eliot attempts to re-establish the continuity of time and shows us glimpses of a salvation to be won through water and fire. We must first pass from the discontinuous to the simultaneous and from the simultaneous to the eternal. In order to protect himself in a world that has lost

[9] *Selected Essays,* p. 358.

its meaning—that evoked by Hermann Hesse in his book *Blick ins Chaos*[10]—Eliot strives to apprehend the unity of human experience. Heights and depths are alike "a succession of moments carried to the point of paroxysm". Borrowed themes or symbols inspire wholly personal variations; Eliot is one of those creative artists who have the gift of transforming their models into anticipated disciples. He gathers up the experience of centuries, yet embodies the spirit of the present age. Heir to the Metaphysical poets, he perceives (as Johnson put it) "hidden resemblances in things apparently unlike"; he "yokes by violence together the most heterogenous ideas". Eliot's mind is "constantly amalgamating disparate experience"; on the other hand, he shows us how "the ordinary man's experience is chaotic, irregular, fragmentary. He falls in love, or reads Spinoza, and those two experiences have nothing to do with each other, or with the noise of the typewriter, or the smell of cooking; in the mind of the poet, these experiences are always forming new wholes."[11]

The Waste Land is a kind of pictured Last Judgment, bringing together simultaneously all manner of things: classical antiquity side by side with scenes of low life; different ages, places, nations, countries, teeming crowds and static solitudes, the mysteries of time and space, everything here (as in Goethe's *Walpürgisnacht*) forming a procession and yet held motionless in suspense. We feel that the poet has transcended the sense of the present, just as when listening to music we cease to hear the sound of individual instruments.

Despite Eliot's religious orthodoxy and his contempt for fortune-telling, I have more than once been tempted to compare some of his cryptic allusions to the Orphism of Nerval. Eliot denies that he has been influenced by Nerval, for the forms adopted by the poet of the *Chimères* are alien to him. But in spite of all that divides Eliot from the Goethean Romanticisms of Gérard Labrunie, they have in common certain features which should not, to my mind, be ignored. They both

[10] From which Eliot borrows in *The Waste Land.*
[11] *The Metaphysical Poets.*

draw inspiration from Indian mysticism and religious tradition; they both discover in the Grail myths the relics of very ancient rituals and primitive beliefs; they both make use of the Tarot characters. Indeed, as early as *Prufrock*, Eliot paraphrased a line from *El Desdichado*:

"J'ai rêvé dans la grotte où nage la sirène"

and it is well known that in *The Waste Land* he quotes

"Le Prince d'Aquitaine à la tour abolie"

not only to preserve it as a relic but because he feels himself to be *"le ténébreux, le veuf, l'inconsolé"* His Tiresias (who is at the same time both male and female, and who is reincarnated in each successive age) recalls Nerval's Peregrinus. (We are reminded of the enigmatic inscription on the tomb of Aelia Laelia Crispis at Bologna: "I am neither man nor woman . . ."[12]

Poetry is here transformed into something strange and disturbing. There is an element of magic, of necromancy. All of us—and everything around us—are under a spell; we are all possessed:

"Here is no water but only rock
Rock and no water and the sandy road
The road winding above among the mountains
Which are mountains of rock without water . . ."[13]

This is a calcined world, void of all signs of life, where the present contains no future, where (as in Kabbalistic Tohu-Bohu) only the debris of a vanished world survive:

"A heap of broken images, where the sun beats,
And the dead tree gives no shelter, the cricket no relief,
And the dry stones on sound of water . . ."[14]

This is the wilderness of Ezekiel's vision; then, by a swift metamorphosis, it becomes the great city of today. Like phan-

[12] cf. Jean Richer, Mercure de France, November 1st 1952.
[13, 14] *The Waste Land.*

toms or puppets, like a shadow-play, like a ghostly *Midsummer Night's Dream,* Elizabeth and Leicester sail down the Thames; Eliot compares their train now to Cleopatra's barge, now to the sordid promiscuity of the "Thames daughters" amidst the oil and tar, the sandwich wrappings and cigarette ends.

In the fifth and last canto all the themes are woven together, all the elements united amidst the air and light and dust, under the title "What the Thunder said." Here we find the journey to Emmaus, the approach to the Chapel Perilous, the "present decay of Eastern Europe",[15] and chaos . . . The recollection of the night of Gethsemane is linked with the myth of the Hanged God. We are at one moment on a Tibetan plain, the next suffering hallucinations in the Antarctic wastes, and then surrounded by the grimacing visions of Hieronymus Bosch . . . But there is method in this madness. For the longed-for sign is granted. After two thousand years of unchanging history, Antiquity reappears. Then the cry of the Walkyries is heard. And amid the thunder—presaging the storm—there rings out the ancient message of the Upanishads :

"Datta, Dahadhvam, Damyata"
(Give, sympathize, control.)

"The awful daring of a moment's surrender" is enough to ensure salvation. Thus the waste land, the ruined land, will be regenerated. This poem of despair ends on a note of expectation; this "season in hell" opens out on to the hope of salvation. And as in the Upanishads, the Sanskrit word *Shantih,* twice repeated, is a ritual evocation of "the peace which passeth all understanding".

* *

The Waste Land comes to us like the codicil of a vanished race, a message sent from beyond the grave, across vast empty spaces, from men long dead. Out of these remains, these fragments, Eliot, like the Byzantine craftsmen of old, has created

[15] i.e. the coming of Bolshevism.

a dazzling mosaic. And like the builders of Venice he embeds in his construction the *spolia opima* of far-off kingdoms.

In an atmosphere of thunderstorm and lucidity, everything becomes an *allegory*. Eliot is an adept at the arbitrary use of the external world. The poet's mind acts as a catalyst; his experiences and impressions combine in various unexpected and special ways. *The Waste Land* has been described as the climax of a line descending from Plato. Like Joyce's *Ulysses* or Valéry's *Jeune Parque,* this poem provides a series of "psychological substitutions" that unfold in the poet's consciousness. By means of apparently incoherent images he expresses the relationship between things whose connecting link had escaped our awareness. And the desolate setting of the poem becomes the exact expression of that blighted world in which we drag out our doubts, our anguish and our apathy. The Elizabethan poets knew this obsession with death. But Eliot is not concerned only with bodily death, nor even that death which a diseased society must undergo; his subject is Death in itself; the death of all creatures, the death of every day, death inherent in all life.

All Eliot's work henceforward comprised a quest for what lies behind appearances. *The Waste Land* has been described as a kind of posthumous poem written by a dead civilization,[16] where the present seems to have no link with the future that may come from it, although it remains submerged under the poignant visions of the past. Eliot seems to make all things dissolve and disintegrate. Against the background of this desolation, the great figures of vanished ages pass like shadow-puppets on a wall. And everything ends with Ophelia's sad, ironic, pathetic farewell:

> "Goodnight, ladies; goodnight, sweet ladies: goodnight!"

What makes Eliot's exorcism so harrowing is that he seems to revive the traces of the past, the "snows of yesteryear" only to make us feel their emptiness. Why do all these ghosts disappoint us? All the cries and clamours, and the sighs of wise men and bards and seers—the Upanishads, Buddha, Ovid,

[16] Stephen Spender, *The Destructive Element,* 1935.

Augustine, Dante, Shakespeare, Kyd, Webster, Baudelaire, Nerval, Wagner, Verlaine—only vibrate for a moment in the sultry air before sinking back into the dust!

In the five parts of *The Waste Land* we discovered "the co-existence of all humanities, the perception of the *simultaneous* raised to the level of the knowledge of the eternal."[17] It is not only a poem about memory, it is, "beyond memory, but thanks to memory, the experience of a mingling of times through which meaning is rediscovered with the immutable".[18] So that the real mystery is that of Time, or, more precisely, the mystery of the insertion of the temporal into the timeless—"which is at the same time the conquest of the Divine and the safeguard of the individual being, threatened with disintegration and ruin by the frenzy of the contemporary world with which, against his will, he is bound up."[19]

Eliot is one of those rare beings who, when they dream, "always know that they are dreaming" (Du Bos). Particular "landscapes of the soul" are then revealed, transfigured, to him; these brief moments of vision contain for him—as for Emerson and Proust—"a depth that obliges us to acknowledge more reality in them than in anything else that we may experience". A mere name is enough to set his imagination flying over the centuries. By a kind of sympathetic magic, the poet penetrates to the heart of "the other", he *is* the other, the protagonist, the deceased, bridging at will the "distance between centuries", taking possession of a dead world, breathing the atmosphere of the past and then emerging in time regained . . .

It is not surprising that, in order to escape from the shame of time and the tyranny of space, Eliot has identified the soul's liberation with this access to the apocalyptic world; for *The Waste Land* prolongs Coleridge's nightmare vision of stagnation. The boredom, the *ennui* he describes is the moral sickness of mankind, out of harmony with himself, of poor humanity vegetating sullenly with passive resignation on its doomed pastures. (All these bewildered, aimless beings seem to be waiting for Godot, like Beckett's Wladimir and Esturgeon). But the

[17, 18, 19] G. A. Astre.

boredom to which Eliot has given dignity is not a personal one; it is, like Baudelaire's, a metaphysical boredom : the boredom of civilization and perhaps that of the cosmos.

Whatever the differences of purpose and plan between Eliot and Joyce one cannot help being struck by certain resemblances between *The Waste Land* on the one hand, and *Ulysses* and *Finnegan's Wake* on the other. In both cases we trace the adventures, the wanderings of a human memory through the Sargasso sea of myths and dreams; they stir the ocean depths, but at the end of their odysseys retain nothing but the fragments of some legendary treasure, some relic which, brought from afar, evokes merely the casual pity of the uninitiated spectator. In both cases, as has been remarked, the loftiest speculations are no more than childish games. In both cases, again, everything is offered to us higgledy-piggledy, yet with consummate discernment. And, from the parallel with ancient myths—Ulysses, Phineas, Galahad, Orestes—the poet draws a subtle music of ideas. In this self-conscious and complex work, the relics of past civilizations are merged and blended in perfect unity; they are gems set by the poet with an art recalling that of medieval craftsmen. We may perhaps suppose that, surveying life from the aesthetic plane, Eliot found nothing more striking than these borrowed cries to emphasize the contrast between the triviality of everyday life and the nobility of the *Idea*. Nor must we ever forget the part played by irony and humour . . .

It is through despair that the poet is led to experience religious emotion. Gerontion, the Magus and the Epiphany, even the old man Simeon—whatever voice Eliot may borrow—always express the same weariness, the same nostalgia, the same mixture of memory and desire, the same resigned anticipation of the joys that the world cannot provide, mingled nevertheless with regret for the things left behind :

"Not for me the martyrdom, the ecstasy of thought and prayer.
Not for me the ultimate vision.
Grant me thy peace . . .
I am tired with my own life and the lives of those after me,

I am dying in my own death and the deaths of those after me,
Let thy servant depart Having seen thy salvation."[20]

That is Simeon's hymn, greeting his Saviour's advent not with cries of rejoicing but by a confession of his own bitter distress. Does an obscure element of Jansenist feeling still persist in Eliot's faith? Is this a painfully subdued gesture of revolt? An old scar, imperfectly healed, which sometimes bleeds? Perhaps doubt and uncertainty are here tortured forms of faith. The universe which emerges from Eliot's visions takes on the character of a forbidden world: beneath a black sun, mineral wildernesses stand motionless, waiting for some unspecified fall of dew. There are no eyes, no exchange of glances beneath these dead stars:

"This is the dead land
This is cactus land
Here the stone images
Are raised, here they receive
The supplication of a dead man's hand
Under the twinkle of a fading star."[21]

How does Eliot return to life from this cactus land, where the Hollow Men, stuffed with straw, whisper together in dried voices,

"quiet and meaningless
As wind in dry grass . . ."

How does he climb up again to the summits of hope and consolation? Is Eliot's pessimism, perhaps, like Emily Dickinson's, in fact that weariness which the spirit experiences under the burden of existence? He is aware, like Valéry, of the close links between suffering and knowledge; the destruction of values is accompanied by a self-awareness striving to reach the highest degree of incandescence. He is in search of some rewarding truth beyond the material values of the contemporary world. Thus in *Animula* he describes the wanderings of the wretched soul

[20] *A Song for Simeon.*
[21] *The Hollow Men.*

drifting helpless from the cradle to the grave. Like his Simeon, he would rejoice at a second death. A second death? let us rather say a second birth, a resurrection. And as always, it is from the sea that this transatlantic sailor receives the sense of renewal. In *Marina* he exclaims, yearning for a fresh departure:

> "what seas what shores what granite islands towards my timbers
> And woodthrush calling through the fog
> My daughter "

4. *The Spiritual Poems*

From Ash Wednesday *to* Four Quartets *(1930-1945)*

NO POETRY is so aptly described as "a spiritual exercise" as that of Eliot. It is not a free-flowing lyricism, but "a highly elaborate, concentrated effort to win freedom from the discontinuous, the temporary, the heterogeneous"; it is an effort "to restore the *self* by the reduction of the diversity of experiences to one single experience, and by the patient rediscovery of its meaning".[1] Yet it is also "religious poetry that is in no way didactic; it does not expound the doctrine or the discipline of faith, but communicates a part of what it has experienced." The lyricism of the poet of *Ash Wednesday* and *Four Quartets* aims at liberating, through the blinding flash of moments of vision, the eternal truth which is at once "in time and out of time".

It might be said of Eliot's God, as of Pierre Emmanuel's, that He is infinitely absent. But is not absence precisely the true "substance" of this poet who constantly strives to detach himself from his work, to destroy any formal unity in which one might be tempted to confine him? Long ravaged by the anguished consciousness of time, he has proved himself capable of truly heroic tenacity. At times his gaze has approached a mystic's vision. Rarely has poetry lingered round a more desolate height. But Eliot is aware that man's mind, "darkened by images," in Maritain's phrase, "cannot penetrate into itself through intelligence alone". For Eliot, as for Maritain, "it is a deadly error to expect poetry to provide the super-substantial nourishment of man." Eliot realized that the Christian

[1] G. A. Astre, *Critique,* April-May 1948.

faith was bound to favour the free development of his true personality; yet he required the deepest humility to renounce the self, "in order to allow the experience of the Divine life to augment, harmonize and illuminate within himself the experience of the poetic state."[2] More than any other poet, he makes us keenly aware of the close links binding poetic creation to the life of the spirit. Eliot's Muse, like Mallarmé's, is a "musician of science." His verse, elliptic, discontinuous, abrupt, irresistibly recalls the sober, condensed poetry of that Bible in which he is so deeply steeped. His phrases, to quote what has been said of the Semitic languages, "strike an idea from its matrix like sparks from a flint." The poet "coagulates and condenses the idea that he wishes to express with a metallic hardness and sometimes a crystalline gleam."[3] The purity of the vocal line is enhanced by the solemn, litany-like intonation.

No doubt Eliot owes his liking for syncopated rhythms to his American origins. In *Four Quartets* he proves more clearly than ever his skill in counterpoint. The harmonious structure of these poems is remarkable. Forswearing his masters, Poe and Baudelaire, Eliot returns by a roundabout route to the long poem, but abandons the narrative. He intermingles subjects; he is discontinuous, but consistent. By inserting unusual elements, by combining vital and unexpected images, Eliot surprises us with a new kind of poetry; his greatest liberties spring from his strictest discipline. Thus he creates "negative beauty", and fulfilling Diderot's wish, "disturbs the ear in order to surprise and satisfy the imagination." He preserves an implicit power, raising his voice only in order to make the ensuing silence more eloquent. His occasional shrill notes, his muffled periods, his deliberate prosaicism alternately vex and delight us. This artist, inimitably and deliberately extreme, succeeds in making abstractions concrete. He creates an atmosphere cloudy with ambiguity, but then illuminates it with a lightning-flash. His images, fused and condensed in an instant, establish a secret order among things which follow no natural sequence. Each poem of

[2] St John of the Cross, translated by Maritain.
[3] L. Massignon, *Pro Psalmis*.

his comprises a moment of life, a living duration which for an instant usurps the inner life of the reader.

Applying the rules of harmony and counterpoint in his own fashion, the poet becomes "one musician among many". Eliot has admitted that it is at the very point when he is most preoccupied with technique that he appears most spontaneous and sincere. Whereas the modern poet offers us everything straight away, Eliot, like the writers of antiquity, plays upon our anticipation. He is obsessed by *birth* and *death,* and not only by the past but by the passage of time; he steeps "the remembrance of the object named in a new atmosphere, and makes you feel surprise at never having heard before some ordinary fragment of speech". (Mallarmé). Eliot has a keen sense of the tonal value of words, sounds and accents, and this gives to a number of his poems the potency of magic spells. He has described as "the auditory imagination" "the feeling for syllable and rhythm, penetrating far below the conscious levels of thought and feeling, invigorating every word; sinking to the most primitive and forgotten, returning to the origin and bringing something back, seeking the beginning and the end."[4] Poems written thus reveal the "music of ideas", music not in the sense of a combination of sounds but by virtue of their internal structure. Eliot is aware that poetry eludes language in so far as it transcends itself; that in fact it *is* that "fine excess" of which Keats wrote. He is aware that the fundamental part of poetry dwells in that most private region of himself, where the essential coincides with his innermost being. He knows that "form" is only that subsoil that must be constantly brought to the surface. Thus his poetry always contains an element of harshness, of strangeness. And for all its echoes of the Classical world, of the Greece of Sophocles and Aeschylus, it none the less remains the expression of a Nordic, Christian tradition. His world has its wuthering heights, its swamps and its stony wildernesses; but the wind that blows over his waste land is a healthy one, and by way of fear he attains intellectual knowledge. Certain moments of vision become the keys to the secret garden: the

[4] *The Music of Poetry.* (Selected Prose, p. 94).

"hyacinth girl" with her wet hair, the gull's cry, the winding staircase, the steps heard on the stair, the light on the kingfisher's wing, the rat "dragging its slimy belly on the bank" . . .

Eliot's poetry seems to fulfil an expectation. It is one of those unforeseen explosions that correspond to the trend of the age and of the newer generations. Does not the power of his work lie in its ability to unsettle the reader from his normal context? The music that accompanies his thought, and is indefinably bound up with it, has an incantatory quality. A certain anguished sense of mystery is common to Supervielle, Kafka and Eliot. Like Joseph of old, they are masters of dream. They are in collusion with the invisible world. But Eliot has no illusions as to the extent of his magic powers; he is aware that poetry can under no circumstances compete with religion, and mistrusts the illusions suggested by the "inner voice". Eliot's lyrical poetry defies conventional analysis; it emerges most clearly from a tangle of contradictions. He leads us through a strait and narrow gate into his private domain, and there "everything is different"; all discrepancies are harmonized under a magic spell. A strange gentleness suffuses even the severe and harsh aspects of Eliot's work. He disturbs and unsettles us only to enslave us more thoroughly with the unearthly powers of his music; so fully, indeed, that the sleeping Caliban in each of us dreams that he wakes up an Ariel; but the calm exaltation that his poetry arouses in us does not claim to be more than "the intoxication of reason". Eliot, like Valéry, turns "abstraction into sensuous pleasure". The emotional force of Eliot's poetry derives from its very structure, but we might hazard the view that he is great in so far as, in defiance of his own theory, he allows his music to open for us the door of the first garden. His poetry is dictated not by the "idea" but by "the nature of that dark embryo" which gradually assumes the form and language of the particular poem.

Eliot reacted against the facile effusions of Romanticism; he gave a new life to English lyrical verse. Detesting both spiritual vagueness and superficial brilliance, he linked feeling closely to the intellect, excluding sentimentality. There is not a passage in *Four Quartets* that can be attributed to chance. The poem progresses towards its "solution" with the strict logic of a problem in mathematics.

Eliot has written: "I know that a poem, or a passage of a poem, may tend to realize itself first as a particular rhythm before it reaches expression in words, and that this rhythm may bring to birth the idea and the image; and I do not believe that this is an experience peculiar to myself."[5] His experiments, like those of Jouve, tend to transform his poems into musical compositions. He says: "The music of a word is, so to speak, at a point of intersection: it arises from its relation first to the words immediately preceding and following it, and indefinitely to the rest of its context; and from another relation, that of its immediate meaning in that context to all the other meanings it had in other contexts, to its greater or less wealth of association."[6] Eliot's writing seems to me to possess those musical qualities of poetic speech whose attributes Valéry has defined so well,[7] although the poet of *Four Quartets* arranges these elements with an art quite different from that of the author of *Le Cimetière Marin*. There is, first, "the sense of the weight and power of words": "a profound, as it were organic, grasp of the function of syntax"; and lastly "feeling for the interconnection of forms". Thanks to this "awareness of the resources of language, of its values and of its articulations", rhythms, accents and intonations have assumed in the composition of each poem "a substantial importance equal to that of the meaning". All Eliot's poems refract an unfamiliar light, as though through a prism. Through skilful artistry he creates a fresh kind of poetic beauty. He has the gift of embodying the dimly felt tendencies of his age in symbols which have a life of their own. His images are no mere flowers of rhetoric, faded through long use; they are, as Dante's allegories were, living associations, concrete particular images linked with a specific identifiable place, with a particular time of day, a particular action, unique and individual circumstances, inalien-

[5], [6] *The Music of Poetry*. (Selected Prose, pp. 60, 66.)

[7] P. Valéry, *Pièces sur l'Art*.

able childhood memories or some specially intense or painful point in the nexus of memories. A gift such as this is more than mastery, and belongs only to the maturity of the most consummate artists who, while they preserve the individual character of their own experience, make from this a symbol of universal significance and, through the transmutation of their problems and griefs, reach that unique state of translucent serenity.

Eliot himself must scarcely be aware of the hallucinatory atmosphere he creates. The objects he describes have a greater density than other objects; the oddness of things is emphasized. The simplest words take on an unfamiliar appearance, a new range of meaning. The transpositions thus brought about prove fertile and stimulating. This "maturing of dream" recalls the mysterious states of mind described by Baudelaire in which "the deepest aspects of life, with all its multiple problems, are revealed all at once in the sight before one's eyes, natural and trivial though this may be—in which anything may become a speaking symbol." This is the miracle of *allegory,* of its analogies and correspondences: "the depths of space, an allegory of the depths of time" . . . and the rest of Baudelaire's words might also be applied to Eliot: "grammar, arid grammar itself, becomes a sort of evocatory witchcraft, words rising up clad in flesh and blood, the substantive in its substantial majesty, the adjective, a transparent garment, clothing it and colouring it like a painter's gaze, and the verb, that angle of motion, which gives the sentence its impetus."[8] Even in his divergence from reality, the poet speaks true, for he uncovers the mysterious side of familiar things and seeks an answer to his anxious questioning, which goes deeper than mere literature. All Eliot's achievement recalls the dreams of one's childhood. A subdued pensive light surrounds him; through the densest darkness, he renews his ascent towards those bare heights where the air is too rarefied to breathe, and where the world of rocks and stones is bathed in an unearthly light. He is in communication with the impalpable. But do not the whispers and gleams that ripple

[8] Baudelaire, *Les Paradis Artificiels, L'Homme-Dieu.*

through his darkness comprise, in themselves, an act of grace? Eliot leads us into a state of meditation in which ordinary words seem of themselves to call forth a sequence of ideas. Associations which we could not have foreseen ensure our complicity. These poetic states, as Jaloux has observed, do not correspond to our normal emotional responses. The poet makes use of "a hereditary consciousness, a fabulous treasure of observations and intuitions bequeathed by thousands of forebears."

An admirable quality of all Eliot's poetry is the masterly way in which the inner melody, the action, theme and metre are united. With him, as with Dante (his favourite master), genius consists in "a poetic intuition which has its source in the inaccessible recesses of the soul, at an exceptional depth", and which Maritain has called "creative innocence". It is, partly, a certain naïvety through which the poet believes not only in things revealed by his poetic experience, but also in every sign revealed by events. It is also that awareness of the wound that set free the creative impulse within him and which, through dreams, through childhood's isolation or some lasting grief, set him apart from other men. It is, lastly, *integrity,* the original purity of his creative emotion, when he touches those deep waters from whose banks he had never strayed far.[9]

Eliot's music moves constantly towards a disconcerting climax, in which discords are resolved. A poem by Eliot suggests something which it is not. Forms suddenly emerge, interrupting the creative current, and are then discarded in favour of others. The *Four Quartets* are full of reminders and repetitions of themes, muffled echoes, sinuous passages, pauses, interlacings and variations. Inspiration means for him self-abnegation, rather than joy; a unique moment "which passes and does not pass"; a flash of lightning which clarifies certain mysteries, patience and passion, multitude and solitude, noise and silence. Through the close interconnection of sound and meaning, such poetry leads us to the intimate heart of things. We feel a sense of unity in multiplicity, the intuition of a presence beyond the reach of Time.

[9] Maritain, *Innocence et Chance de Dante.*

Eliot has written: "The use of recurring themes is as natural to poetry as to music. There are possibilities for verse which bear some analogy to the development of a theme by different groups of instruments; there are possibilities of transitions in a poem comparable to the different movements of a symphony or a quartet; there are possibilities of contrapuntal arrangement of subject-matter."[10]

In *Ash Wednesday* there is already present what has been called "allegorical counterpoint". As Louis Bolle has observed, "in the heart of this twilight, purgatorial atmosphere, a light dawns: . . . the sense of history, linked with that of the Incarnation, emerges clearly." Henceforward we perceive "the stages of a vision growing constantly more clear-cut, conveyed in language constantly more flexible." After the "rocky desert" of *The Waste Land,* after the even more barren landscape of *The Hollow Men*—the dead land, the cactus land, land of the prickly pear—*Ash Wednesday* throws open the door of the garden of consolation. Time forms the subject of the first cycle, as it later forms the theme of *Four Quartets:*

> "Because I cannot hope to turn again . . .
> Consequently I rejoice, having to construct something
> Upon which to rejoice."

Nevertheless Eliot accepts the restraint and the great hope inherent in Christianity:

> "Redeem the time, Redeem the dream . . .
> The token of the word unheard, unspoken . . ."

When we listen to the plainsong of *Ash Wednesday,* with its prose sections, its chants and its litanies, when I vizualize beneath Elijah's juniper-tree

> "the three leopards . . . having fed to satiety
> On my legs, my heart, my liver and that which had been contained
> In the hollow round of my skull,"

[10] *The Music of Poetry.* Selected Prose, p. 67.

when we gaze at Our Lady of Silences, Rose of Memory, Rose of Forgetfulness, in her white gown beneath the yew trees; when we perceive, in that place of solitude where three dreams meet, amidst the blue rocks and the thorn trees and the sea smell and the plovers' flight, that Blessed Mother and that Sister who is at once the Spirit of the Fountain and the Spirit of the Sea, then we seem to behold a vision of the spirit of Old and New England, a spirit more delicate than Ariel. But surely we are also in that flower-filled valley, hollowed out in the bosom of the mountains, described by Dante in Canto XXIII of the *Purgatorio*? There, in the sunset glow of the Angelus, at the holy hour of Compline, amidst trees and flowers, there is heard the chanting of *Salve Regina*; there, amongst the lilies, shines out that "Rose in whom the Word was made flesh." She is the Virgin of the Rocks, the Blessed Lady in whom time and eternity meet. She is the Light of the Seal, the One who redeems the Time and the Dream. Because the poet has no hope of returning

> "there, where trees flower, and springs flow . . ."

he rejoices, in penitence, that things are as they are; he renounces "the blessed face and the voice" because he "does not hope to turn again" . . .

New England landscapes are often recognizable in *Ash Wednesday*. Similarly, in *Four Quartets,* we see a sequence of images of migration, pinning down past and present or, even more, a series of soundings enabling us to explore time through history, until the spiral evolution of man is revealed. Eliot himself has said that the four cantos gradually began to assume a relation to the four elements and to the four seasons; thus we have air, and early summer, for *Burnt Norton;* earth, and the end of summer, for *East Coker*; water and autumn for *The Dry Salvages*; fire and midwinter for *Little Gidding*. It goes without saying that these parallels should not be over-emphasized. (In *East Coker,* the end of autumn and Spring are intermingled.) The final revelation, however, is that when Man enters the garden of the past and searches out its history, he arrives at the same garden from which he had first emerged.[11]

This is also suggested, with a slightly different meaning, by the two epigrams from Heraclitus: "Though the Word (Logos) is common to all, most men live as though each of them had his own particular wisdom." And: "The way up and the way down are one and the same way." Plurality exists in sensation, unity in thought. From this arises the concept of an immanent Mind in the world, already implicit in the humorous poem "Mr Eliot's Sunday Service".[12]

But to return to *Four Quartets,* which is undoubtedly one of the summits of Eliot's achievement and one of the crowning glories of Symbolist aethetics. As Wagner said: "A poet's most accomplished work must be that which in its final shape would form a perfect musical whole." And Mallarmé, teaching us the art of breathing new life into recollections and the necessity of recreating everything through memories, was certainly the precursor of these "mystical metamorphoses" in which things preserve the essence of the past. The rhythm of the words succeeds in suggesting what language had hitherto seemed incapable of rendering. The poet leads us into secret places where his spirit (and his reader's) rediscovers the sources of its inner life.

Helen Gardner[13] makes a close analysis of *Four Quartets.* In her opinion, the five movements suggest the five acts of a spiritual drama, a dialectical process of thought (contrast, return, then patient progress) leads to the recurrence of themes, orchestrated in different ways. The opening is usually built up on contradictions which must then be resolved. The second

[11] *Burnt Norton,* composed in the autumn of 1935, first appeared in *Collected Poems* (1909-1935), published April 2nd 1936. The first separate edition of *Burnt Norton* appeared on February 20th 1941. The other Quartets, written between 1939 and 1942, appeared in *The New English Weekly: East Coker* on March 21st 1940, *The Dry Salvages* on February 27th 1941, and *Little Gidding* on October 15th 1942. The first collective edition of *Four Quartets* was that of Harcourt, Brace & Co, New York, May 11th 1943; it was followed by that of Faber & Faber, London, October 31st 1944.

[12] cf. G. Williamson, op. cit.

[13] *The Art of T. S. Eliot,* London, 1949.

movement (similar in each Quartet) opens with a lyrical passage, followed by a passage of familiar speech; the idea, first treated in a symbolic way, is then developed and applied to a specific example, on conversational level. The third movement contains the core of the poem, its essential meaning, as a prelude to reconciliation. "It is an exploration at the same time as a fusion of the two central ideas."

Helen Gardner summarizes the themes of the Quartets in the following three phrases: the relationship between duration and the timeless; the sense of history; the mysteries of the Incarnation and the Redemption. One might, however, observe about certain explanations of Eliot's poetry what he himself has said of the treatises which claim to expound Mallarmé's meaning: that they add nothing to his enjoyment of the poetry; some disclose the accidental sources of the poet's inspiration, which may be interesting but bear no relation to the poem itself; others offer a philosophical interpretation which is always inferior to the poem; and yet all this does not imply that the poetry has no meaning, or that he could enjoy it if he knew it had no meaning.[14]

About the *Four Quartets*, every possible comment has been made since critics first sought to "drain" in prose the elusive marshland of his dreams. Nevertheless, let us venture to enter the mysterious manor of Burnt Norton, about which even the poet himself seems rather ill informed.[15] The building, which was burnt down in former times, stands in Gloucestershire, in the very heart of England. We are now in the rose garden, which bears a certain resemblance to the Persian poet's Gulistan. The "unheard music" in this garden represents the enigmatic longings with which memory is obsessed. It is an autumn garden, filled with echoes of footfalls:

> "Down the passage which we did not take
> Towards the door we never opened
> Into the rose garden . . . Shall we follow?

[14] *Scylla and Charybdis,* lecture published in French.

[15] Although he lived near there for a while, in 1934. The house was formerly known as "The Burnt House".

Quick, said the bird, find them, find them
Round the corner . . ."

And like Proust, Eliot records these scenes of "our first world":

"dignified, invisible,
Moving without pressure, over the dead leaves,
In the autumn heat, through the vibrant air.
And the bird called, in response to
The unheard music hidden in the shrubbery,
And the unseen eye-beams crossed, for the roses
Had the look of flowers that are looked at."

Thus they moved in a formal pattern

"Along the empty alley, into the box circle,
To look down into the drained pool."

Then, suddenly, the dry pool

". . . was filled with water out of sunlight,
And the lotus rose, quietly, quietly,
The surface glittered out of heart of light . . .
. . . Then a cloud passed, and the pool was empty.
Go, said the bird, for the leaves were full of children,
Hidden excitedly, containing laughter.
Go, go, go, said the bird: human kind
Cannot bear very much reality."[16]

As has already been pointed out, the significance of the Rose Garden vision[17] is made even clearer in *The Family Reunion,* and it has already existed potentially in earlier poems such as *The Waste Land, Ash Wednesday* and *Coriolanus*. It is the equivalent of "the still point of the turning world" and the "movement inside and outside time" which so often reappear in Eliot's poetry.

In spite of his hostility to D. H. Lawrence's philosophical

[16] This phrase had already appeared in *Murder in the Cathedral.*

[17] Eliot speaks of the Metaphysical poets as feeling their thought "as immediately as the odour of a rose." cf the lines in the Roman. de la Rose:

*"L'odeur des roses savoree
M'entra jusque en la coree"*

ideas and beliefs, Eliot observed that Lawrence had the power of communicating in flashes of vision the sensual fulness of the moment.[18] In *Burnt Norton* Eliot did not only evoke Lawrence's Rose-garden; he also apparently borrowed several of the basic images of this *Quartet* from the Preface written by Lawrence for the American edition of *New Poems* (1920).[19] Strange, indeed, is the long history of the rose; once sung by Hafiz and Saadi, its scent has pervaded the ages, it was endowed with rich mystical significance by the Sufi poets and those of the Christian Middle Ages, by troubadours and by court poets, by Dante and the *Roman de la Rose*. And then, via D. H. Lawrence—and more surprisingly Proust himself—this rose, contrasted with the lotus, appears in Eliot's *Quartets*. What could be more unexpected than this revelation of affinities between Eliot and some of his contemporaries whose tendencies seem so remote from his own! Giorgio Melchiori has also commented on certain resemblances between Eliot's vision and that of Proust. Referring to the lily ponds of Vivonne, Melchiori observes: "In three writers, first Proust, then D. H. Lawrence, and lastly T. S. Eliot, the moment of absolute clarity, of rapture and fulfilment is expressed by the same symbol—the lotus flower. The flower of oblivion becomes the flower of memory; it arouses that sensation of physical and spiritual ecstasy, of luminous and languid beauty, that they wished to communicate. And it holds time suspended . . ." The lotus, as a result of the significance it had acquired in the pages of Proust and Lawrence, created the atmosphere in which the fundamental theme of *Four Quartets* could be expressed—that of the moment of Incarnation. And it also introduced the element of timelessness.

The mysterious kinship which, spanning seas and linguistic frontiers, links the lily ponds of the Vivonne with the "lotos

[18] F. Fergusson (*Hound and Horn,* 1933) pointed out a borrowing from Lawrence's *Rainbow* in *The Waste Land.* See also *The Shadow in the Rose Garden,* a story by Lawrence, pointed out by L. L. Martz: "The Wheel of the Point: aspects of Imagery and Theme in Eliot's later poetry", *The Sewanee Review,* Winter 1947. Reprinted in *T. S. Eliot, A selected critique,* pub. L. Anger, New York, 1948.

[19] Essay reprinted in 1936 in *The Phoenix* (posthumous collection).

pool" of Burnt Norton or the house at Combray with that of East Coker, represents a coincidence more significant than all uncertain assessments of influence; but such relations are not always easy to pin down in print.

To reiterate, it is Time—which has obsessed poets from Villon to Wordsworth, and which Bergson said poets have often *felt* more truly than philosophers—that provides one basic theme of the three following Quartets. It is Time that makes our days "divided and disappointing", past, present, future, always the same obstacle, the same impediment! Eliot dreams of a timeless moment whose plenitude abolishes duration, that eternal instant of which Kierkegaard and Proust spoke. Such moments release us from any inner external compulsion; they are surrounded, haloed by "a white light still and moving." The second movement of *Burnt Norton* provides a vision of the world as seen by a man in beatific ecstasy. In freeing our souls from bodily limitations, this light reveals the true meaning of created things. Eliot suggests that the "white light still and moving" is not of merely earthly origin. It brings to life a new world and illuminates the "old made explicit." Thus the story of a single human life and the story of a nation appear, suddenly lit up by a flash of winter lightning or in the flames of a modern Pentecost.

The poet's meditation assumes a new aspect, pointing "to one end, which is always present."

> "Garlic and sapphires in the mud
> Clot the bedded axle-tree.
> The trilling wire in the blood
> Sings below inveterate scars
> Appeasing long forgotten wars,
> The dance along the artery
> The circulation of the lymph
> Are figured in the drift of stars
> Ascend to summer in the tree . . ."[20]

[20] In the second movement of *Burnt Norton* we recognized not only the paraphrase of Mallarmé's words: *Tonnerre et rubis aux moyeux,* but the echo of the whole poem: *"M'introduire dans ton histoire . . ."*

If everything is always present, where are we to find the time that will console us? The poet tells us—neither in action nor in old age, but in the purification of thought, in light, in the upward path.

> "Time and the bell have buried the day,
> The black cloud carries the sun away.
> Will the sunflower turn to us, will the clematis
> Stray down, bend to us; tendril and spray
> Clutch and cling?
> Chill
> Fingers of yew be curled
> Down on us? After the kingfisher's wing
> Has answered light to light, and is silent, the light is still
> At the still point of the turning world."[21]

The poet seeks out those moments that prolong the simplicity of childhood and of our beginnings. And since his concern is with words, with speech, Eliot seeks his "way of illumination" in the creation of a work of art which will provide a microcosm of the universe.

> ". . . Words, after speech, reach
> Into the silence. Only by the form, the pattern,
> Can words or music reach
> The stillness, as a Chinese jar still
> Moves perpetually in its stillness."

* *

> "Sudden in a shaft of sunlight
> Even while the dust moves
> There rises the hidden laughter
> Of children in the foliage
> Quick now, here, now, always—
> Ridiculous the waste sad time
> Stretching before and after."

* *

[21] Blake's Sunflower and Tennyson's Yew are also symbols of death.

East Coker is the name of a village in Somerset, near Yeovil. As we noted earlier, Eliot's distant ancestors lived here for several generations : Andrew Eliot, who settled near Boston and left many descendants, emigrated from here in 1677. By returning to this land of his fathers, the author of the *Quartets* completed one of his four pilgrimages, one of those voyages into his family's past, into his own past, by which he seems to close a cycle or at least trace the circular ascent of a spiral. And this is why, paraphrasing the motto of Mary Queen of Scots, he exclaims in his turn :

> "In my beginning is my end
> . . . In my end is my beginning."

These are the first and last words of the poem. This nostalgic pilgrimage to places now deconsecrated, to the crumbling stones of an ancestral home ("In succession Houses rise and fall . . .") might seem to us like a new version of Ronsard's *Forêt de Gastine,* Hugo's *Tristesse d'Olympio* or Valéry's *Cimetière Marin,* were it not that the old commonplace is transfigured by the rhythm and tone and by the introduction of a religious accent which raises the curve of our spiral, suddenly transforming it into an ascent of Mount Carmel. The poetry of *East Coker,* written for Good Friday 1940, is imbued with that chill darkness which can be identified alternately with a foreboding of disaster and the "dark night" of St John of the Cross.

The descent into the gloom of the London Underground (in the third section of *Burnt Norton*) has also symbolized a descent into the "night" of the mystics. The allusion becomes even more explicit in *East Coker*. The poet bids his soul

> "wait without hope
> For hope would be hope for the wrong thing . . ."

These passages are echoed in *Little Gidding* with the Dante-like terzettos which close to the second part and the prosaic lines which open the third. In accordance with a system of alternation, the themes are taken up on varying planes. The fourth movement, as in *The Waste Land,* is always a brief lyric; the fifth recalls or resolves all the themes and *motifs.* For the *Quartets* are not composed about a subject, the subject lies within the poem. "A poem may, in fact, include several subjects, each of which might be expressed in different terms . . . For the poet's task may have been to harmonize several subjects having between them no connection formulable in abstract terms. And from their union there arises, not another subject, but the poem itself." In each Quartet the tone is straightway evident; the attack is open and clearcut. Through all the variations of Eliot's polyphonic prosody, there sounds the multiple echo of one image; his music corresponds to the "starts of consciousness" and seems, to borrow Jouve's phrase, "linked to the circulation of the blood". This is indeed that "inspired mathematics" that the Imagists had dreamed of. It contains a good measure of that wit, those conceits characteristic of Milton and Marvell, for Eliot unites the austerity of Lucretius with Catullus' lightness of touch. Even the quotations inserted in the matrix of his verse take on a new significance; they become the pretext for, or subject of, highly individual fugues. In this way too Stravinsky and Picasso transform their borrowings, making something startlingly original out of their pastiches.

Such is the fourth movement, in which we hear echoes of the Metaphysical poets and of Sir Thomas Browne's bitter reflection, in *Religio Medici*: "For the World, I count it not an Inn, but an Hospital; and a place not to live, but to die in." If *Burnt Norton* is the past, *East Coker* is the starting-point. For Eliot, "home is where one starts from." And since the time foretold by Ecclesiastes has now arrived,

> "a time for the wind to break the loosened pane,
> And to shake the wainscot where the field-mouse trots
> And to shake the tattered arras woven with a silent motto,
> In my beginning is my end . . ."

the poet, who refuses to put his faith in horoscopes, necromancers, spirit-raisers or astrologers, allows himself at night to be bewitched by the spirit of a place. Thus the past becomes clear to him, he is endowed with that mysterious sense which makes "things that have been" present for ever in the records of time. Then, as in those German folk tales in which the phantom merrymaking of an accursed parish excommunicated by the Church comes to life at midnight for a single moment, and then sinks underground, so the ghosts of the villagers of East Coker dance once again before the eyes of their distant descendant, mysteriously murmuring the words that Sir Thomas Elyot himself had written here in 1531 concerning

> "The association of man and woman
> In daunsyng, signifying matrimonie . . ."

Darkness and light here provide the key to man's fate. "The darkness shall be the light." The tone of the poem becomes more and more elevated. Now that "the houses are all gone under the sea" and "the dancers are all gone under the hill" the poet, grown old, realizes that

> "Here and there does not matter
> We must be still and still moving
> Into another intensity
> For a further union, a deeper communion
> Through the dark cold and the empty desolation,
> The wave cry, the wind cry, the vast waters
> Of the petrel and the porpoise . . ."

* *

Very different is the third Quartet, *The Dry Salvages.* Its name refers to that group of rocks off the coast of Massachusetts, probably once called in French *"Les Trois Sauvages."* Here we breathe, as we breathed in *Marina,* the tang of the Northern seas, and feel that deep ground-swell which now mingles with the bitter conflicts of the submarine world. *The Dry Salvages* contrasts the river which is "within us" with the sea, which is "all about us". These are the two forces which have most powerfully inspired Eliot's rhythms. Is not "the river" the Mississippi, as a child's imagination saw it in contrast with the Atlantic coastline of New England? Writing in a St Louis newspaper in 1930, Eliot declared that the region around the Missouri and the Mississippi, where he had spent his childhood, had made a deeper impression on him than any other part of the world.

Thus he feels himself once again carried away by the song of the great river on whose banks he had lived as a child. He dreams of those "sullen, untamed and intractable" waters, which appeared to him in the guise of a "strong brown god," of that "river within us" :

> "His rhythm was present in the nursery bedroom,
> In the rank ailanthus of the April dooryard,
> In the smell of grapes on the autumn table,
> And the evening circle in the winter gaslight."

Eliot rediscovers the sea of his youth on the coast of Cape Ann and its granite shore, its seaweed, its driftwood, its sea-anemones, all its "many voices", all its laments, and the note of the bell-buoy and the "groaner", and the "ground-swell, that is and was from the beginning . . .

> "The river is within us, the sea is all about us :
> The sea is the land's edge also, the granite
> Into which it reaches, the beaches where it tosses
> Its hints of earlier and other creation :
> The starfish, the horseshoe crab, the whale's backbone . . ."

It is as if the bare bones of our planet had suddenly been revealed on this wild beach, on the edge of the primeval waters. We are reminded of certain images of Donne's. These are exegeses on Death : the death of earth, of water, and of air . . . Our memories are thus filled with jetsam :

> "For most of us, there is only the unattended
> Moment, the moment in and out of time,
> The distraction fit, lost in a shaft of sunlight,
> The wild thyme unseen, or the winter lightning
> Or the waterfall, or music heard so deeply
> That it is not heard at all, but you are the music

While the music lasts. These are only hints and guesses,
Hints followed by guesses; and the rest
Is prayer, observance, discipline, thought and action."

After contrasting the River with the Sea, the lifestream flowing within us with that surrounding us, childhood and duration, heredity and environment, the poet was bound to seek a spiritual harbour. He chose Little Gidding, an obscure and lonely hamlet in Huntingdonshire, not far from Cambridge. Here Nicholas Ferrer, a friend of the poet George Herbert's, settled in 1626 with his family to found a kind of religious community, living the life of prayer and contemplation, singing psalms and humbly serving God. Here, too, came Charles I, the "broken King" pursued by Cromwell, in the middle of the night, in search of a precarious refuge. It is not surprising that such a place should have inspired Eliot's finest lyric. *Little Gidding,* the last movement of his fourfold poem, is set under the sign of Pentecost and of the Royal Rose which rules over fire and blood and leads us to the final ecstasy, the apotheosis, when the fire of Purgatory becomes Dante's Rose of Paradise. Here conqueror and conquered find themselves united in the mysterious communion of inward experience. And here, at this point in history, the cycle is completed: *in my end is my beginning.*

No longer do we feel only the wind of death; the wind of resurrection blows through *Little Gidding*:

"If I think of a king at nightfall,
Of three men, and more, on the scaffold
And a few who died forgotten
In other places, here and abroad,
And of one who died blind and quiet,
Why should we celebrate
These dead men more than the dying?[22]
It is not to ring the bell backward
Nor is it an incantation
To summon the spectre of a Rose.

[22] Charles I, Milton the Puritan, Archbishop Laud, Strafford and the Roman Catholic Crashaw are here united and reconciled.

And all shall be well and
All manner of thing shall be well
By the purification of the motive
In the ground of our beseeching.

* *

In these last poems (and in particular in *Little Gidding*) Eliot rejoins the tradition of the Metaphysical poets, and even—further back than Crashaw, Donne and Marvell—those old English mystics such as Julian of Norwich, from whom he quotes a few words; like Hopkins, he revived their racy language with its alliterations, assonances and analogies. Each of Eliot's poems refracts, as though through different media, one single type of beauty which is his alone. This is what makes his art so valuable; these are poems such as no one before him had written or could have written. He makes us share in his conflicts, his expectations, his anguished pauses and his final satisfying solutions.

"We shall not cease from exploration
And the end of our exploring
Will be to arrive where we started
And know the place for the first time.
Through the unknown, remembered gate
When the last of earth left to discover
Is that which was the beginning;
At the source of the longest river
The voice of the hidden waterfall
And the children in the apple-tree
"Not known, because not looked for
But heard, half-heard, in the stillness
Between two waves of the sea."

Although Eliot has written a number of short poems since *Little Gidding*—such as the moving "For the Indian soldiers who died far from their country"—the *Fourth Quartet* can be said to mark both the climax of his work and his finest achievement, constituting the true Paradise of his Divine Comedy; we had long wandered through the sulphurous circles of its

Inferno and Purgatory. And since each of the preceding Quartets had united aesthetics and metaphysics, it is fitting that in this "Time Regained", as in Proust's, the poet should have bequeathed us his *ars poetica*. It is fitting, again, that by uniting in a single evocation all his "masters of language", he should, like Dante, have called forth from the shadows a figure that is Dantean both in imagery and in tone, and in whom the characteristics of Arnaut Daniel, Brunetto Latini, Mallarmé and various others are blended.

"In the uncertain hour before the morning
Near the ending of interminable night
At the recurrent end of the unending
After the dark dove with the flickering tongue
Had passed below the horizon of his homing
While the dead leaves still rattled on like tin
Over the asphalt where no other sound was
Between three districts whence the smoke arose
I met one walking, loitering and unhurried
As if blown towards me like the metal leaves
Before the urban dawn wind unresisting.
And as I fixed upon the down-turned face
That pointed scrutiny with which we challenge
The first-met stranger in the waning dusk
I caught the sudden look of some dead master
Whom I had known, forgotten, half recalled
But one and many; in the brown baked features
The eyes of a familiar compound ghost
Both intimate and unidentifiable.
So I assumed a double part, and cried
And heard another's voice cry : 'What, are *you* here?'
Although we were not. I was still the same,
Knowing myself, yet being someone other . . ."[23]

Such, in its Dantesque terzetti, is the description of a dawn encounter in Kensington towards the end of an air raid. In the mysterious stranger Eliot recognizes the figure whose concern was "To purify the dialect of the tribe".

[23] cf. Nerval *Je suis l'autre* (I am the other) and Rimbaud *Je est un autre* (*I* is another).

This time, the poet had kept his tryst with History. For Eliot,

> "... A people without history
> Is not redeemed from time, for history is a pattern
> Of timeless moments. So, while the light falls
> On a winter's afternoon, in a secluded chapel
> History is now and England."

This declaration seems to be an answer to former regrets, to Gerontion's remorse when he lamented the fact that he

> "was neither at the hot gates
> Nor fought in the warm rain ..."

but had skulked in his "decayed house", had in fact missed History, that embodiment of the eternal in the present.

Eliot's poems are remarkable for that ripeness of the intelligence which is inseparable from the unfolding of a man's entire personality and the development of his sensibility through a long sequence of remembered emotions. He establishes an "analogy between a moment of the duration of the self and a moment of the duration of things." His living intimacy with the great spirits of the past is no straightforward historic relationship. For he apprehends history as a future presence within the heart of total simultaneity; he considers past events as still taking place today and as about to take place tomorrow. Perhaps he thinks like Master Eckhardt that the Word is continually reborn in nature and in history.

* *

In 1911 Eliot had attended Bergson's lectures, and had criticized them, for *real duration* did not seem to him the last word on the problem. On the other hand, he has denied having read the whole of Proust. I do not imagine that he has studied Kierkegaard. Yet these are the names that spring to mind when one reads *Four Quartets*. But Eliot is still closer to the teaching of St Augustine[24] or the Hindu tradition, with its concept of a

[24] I have in mind, too, St Augustine's comparison of History to "an uninterrupted musical flux, following the risings and fallings that seem calculated, hurried or slowed down, of the melodic order: *velut magnum carmen ineffabilis modulatoris*". Claudel in *La Liturgie,* cf. also *L'Eglise et la Sainte Vierge.*

"still centre" within a "turning world", a sort of ideal *fermata,* mathematically pure; not unlike the "unmoved mover" of the Scholastics and of Dante. Such comparisons might appear startling, had not Eliot himself stated that we cannot separate criticism from metaphysics, any more than we can distinguish aesthetic criticism from moral and social criticism, so that starting from literary criticism we suddenly find ourselves in quite another domain. It must be remembered that Eliot in his youth felt drawn to philosophy, that he even wrote a thesis about Belief, and above all that he devoted two years of his life to studying the Vedas, the Upanishads, and the Bhagavad-Gita. It is as though his Christian faith were grafted on to a basis of Hindu philosophy.[25] Perhaps Eliot feels like the Indian sage that only the Invisible, the Imperceptible, the Supreme, without form or colour, really exisits. All is Maya, illusion. Spirit must be delivered from matter. Only Brahma exists! For Eliot, action brings release. The world is a cycle; the end is in the beginning. Creative force is always action. The world, like the waves of the ocean, now surges and now sinks down. Thus by ever deeper soundings we must grasp, in its primal, uncategorized state, that inner life that springs up unchanged. We must remember, too, that Eliot has been a constant reader of Spinoza; Denis Saurat has also suggested links with Malebranche and Berkeley. But in the case of a poet, Eliot's own words should be remembered: "I doubt whether belief proper enters into the activity of a great poet, *qua* poet. That is, Dante *qua* poet did not believe or disbelieve the Thomist cosmology or theory of the soul; he merely made use of it, or a fusion took place between his initial emotional impulses and a theory, for the purpose of making poetry."[26]

Eliot believes, in contrast with Poe, that: "Yet it is only in poem of some length that a variety of moods can be expressed; for a variety of moods requires a number of different themes or

[25] The third section of *The Dry Salvages* evokes the Dialogue between Krishna and Arjuna.

[26] "Shakespeare and Seneca." Selected Essays, p. 138.

subjects, related either in themselves or in the mind of the poet."[27]

In this poetry, the fusion between Eliot's beliefs and his emotions has taken place. He has achieved what Coleridge called "the balance or reconcilement of opposite or discordant qualities," of the idea with the image, the general with the concrete, sameness with difference. He has revealed at the heart of things "a past whose absence had more reality than their presence". He has made his dreams palpable to us.

For Eliot, the greatness of a poem is connected not only with those "touchstones" of which Matthew Arnold wrote, but also with the way the poet composes certain passages which are less intense, though of a vital structural importance. In the *Four Quartets* Eliot passes with consummate skill from incantatory lyrical fragments to prosaic interludes; the tempo of these recitatives constrasts with that of the pure lyrical passages that precede and follow them, providing a great variety of tone, full of subtle nuances. In each Quartet, the fifth movement contains a recapitulation and a resolution of all the themes—above all *Little Gidding,* which summarizes and embodies the themes of the preceding Quartets. It is, indeed, a grand conception that inspires these "spiritual exercises", which transcend poetry, and which have been compared to Beethoven's last quartets, where the composer goes "beyond music".

Here the painter's world and that of the musician are united by delicate touches to the very stuff the poet's dreams are made of. In this strange amalgam of what was, what is and what is not, we perceive the continuous passage and transformation of all forms of things, of all the "productions of Time". Each of Eliot's poems in turn necessarily sheds light on a new aspect of the same mysterious world, other fragments of which we already know. . . "This realm (of which works of art are fragmentary glimpses) is the poet's soul, his true soul, that one of all his souls which is his truest homeland, but where he only dwells for rare moments. That is why the light that shines there, the colours that gleam there, the figures that move there, are *intellectual*

[27] "From Poe to Valéry", *To Criticize the Critic,* p. 34.

light and colours and beings. Inspiration is the moment when the poet can penetrate into this innermost soul."[28]

Eliot's vision is of this kind, always recognizable, homogeneous, allegorical and precise—as though traced from some mysterious drawing quivering in his heart. The girl who "weaves the sunlight in her hair" and the one whose brown locks mingle with the lilac; the song of the hermit thrush and the plover's call and the gulls' cry in the wind; the undersea currents, the sea swell, the bell-buoy, the drifting corpses; the sunlit snowy slopes, the hyacinths, the white-robed Lady standing among rocks and yew-trees, by a spring; the Rose and the Lotos—for Eliot these are, we realise, symbolic images, no less than the yellow fog and sordid streets of the "Unreal City". For this reason, we are moved by each recurrence of these familiar images, each return of earlier themes, each evocation of these hallowed shrines; for in them we recognize, as in a leit motiv, elements essential to the poet's being, recurrent emotions, significant memories, appropriate apparitions by means of which we glimpse the very core and essence of his consciousness. I cannot listen to these *Quartets* without thinking of Vinteuil's Sonata and Septet, as Proust describes them. For here too we have those "insistent, fleeting themes, which fade only to reappear, and which though almost dissociated, are at other times, though remaining vague, so urgent and so close, so inward and so organic, so visceral that they seem not so much to repeat a theme as to revive a neurosis."[29] Eliot's poetry, like music, communicates the "qualitative essence" of another being's sensations; it gives new relevance to many disparate elements, which it fuses and transforms and whose true colour it reveals. Each new poem is an unfamiliar utterance, different from anything we could have envisaged, and yet each time we recognize certain familiar, personal and private themes, words and images, which are Eliot's own and which illuminate his mysterious inner world for us, disclosing part of the secret of his inalienable self. At times Eliot develops a single theme through several varia-

[28] Marcel Proust, *Contre Sainte-Beuve,* pp. 388-389.
[29] Marcel Proust, *La Prisonnière,* p. 159.

tions, changing the rhythm, then presenting it in its original form; but it is precisely when he seeks to appear different that we perceive his basic continuity beneath apparent dissimilarities, for, searching his own consciousness with the full force of his creative effort, he "attains his own essence at such deep levels that whatever question is asked him, he will answer with the same accent, his own"—a *unique* accent, which Proust would describe as "a proof of the irreducibly individual existence of the soul."[30]

[30] Proust. *La Prisonnière,* p. 256.

5. *The Poetic Dramas*

From The Rock *to* The Elder Statesman

WHAT WRITER, whether novelist or poet, has not dreamed of transporting his visions, his imagined characters on to the stage, and of submitting them to the glare of the footlights? What seemed to qualify Eliot, from *Prufrock* onwards, for an attempt to restore poetic drama was that his verse is never too "remote from ordinary speech" and, however hermetic some of his lines may be, he has never—even while exploring the "musical possibilities" of poetic diction—lost sight of the relation between prosody and the spoken language; he has even, following the example of certain predecessors, attempted to follow the evolution of common speech. (And as he observes, dramatic prose is no less artificial than verse.) Eliot refers legitimately to the example of Shakespeare, who adapted his form to the very tone of conversation, who, in a word, created a means of expression in which "everything can be said that has to be said," whether sublime or prosaic, with ease and grace.[1] Eliot goes so far as to justify Molière's Monsieur Jourdain, who is amazed to learn that he speaks prose; for the spoken language differs as much from the written language as from verse. Eliot may use everyday language and themes, yet imperceptibly he raises them, by

[1] Ian Bevan writes: "A few years ago, T. S. Eliot spent hours at a time beating a toy drum; he was seeking rhythms for his poems. This drum-beating resulted in a fragmentary, unactable play, *Sweeney Agonistes.* Eliot came to the conclusion that his drum had led him to write verse that could not be spoken as fast as he would have liked; so he put away his drum and has not beaten it since. But he has gone on writing plays and has achieved success." (*Figaro Littéraire,* September 2nd 1950.)

cadence and allusion, to the heights of Greek tragedy. He rejects, however, the blank verse of the Elizabethans, too remote from the rhythms of contemporary speech, basing himself rather on the traditional metre of *Everyman*. It is strange that he should have waited so long before starting to write drama, for which his talents seemed peculiarly fitted, and which he had broached in the dialogue fragments *Sweeney Agonistes* and *Coriolan*. These had already revealed his power of expression, his satiric genius, his ability to bring alive bizarre characters, sprung from his burlesque imagination or his disillusioned sense of humour: apeneck Sweeney, Princess Volupine, perhaps a descendant of Ben Jonson's Volpone; Grishkin, whose "Russian eye is underlined for emphasis"; Burbank with his Baedeker, de Bailhache with his dreams, and Phlebas the Phoenician, and the Smyrna merchant. . .

In spite of his admiration for the Elizabethan dramasists,[2] Eliot did not hesitate to disclaim their aesthetic theories, at least in part, and to concur with Sir Philip Sidney's denunciation of the lowness of the English stage in 1580. The arbitrary juxtaposition of the comic and the tragic was certainly based on that lack of concentration of which human nature gives constant proof. This failing had to be overcome, not pandered to; an audience whose attention can be fixed on "pure tragedy" or "pure comedy" gives proof of higher qualities. Thus for Eliot, Racine's *Bérénice* represents "the summit of civilization in tragedy." (It is, he considers, in some sort a Christian tragedy, in which devotion to the cause of the State is substituted for devotion to God's law). The doctrine of the unity of feeling, which Sidney had already demanded and which is more important that the other three, was in a way to triumph none the less, since it was embodied in *Coriolanus, Volpone,* and *The Way of the World*.

It has been said that "a work of art owes its concreteness to the plurality of the artist's intentions". The dictum seems especially appropriate to Eliot's various literary activities. In

[2] Eliot, as is well known, gave a fresh impetus to the study of the Elizabethan theatre.

1919, in an essay on "Rhetoric and Poetic Drama," he had outlined his dramatic theories. He returned to this topic in 1928, in an ingenious "Dialogue on Dramatic Poetry". More recently (1950) he has given us the study called "Poetry and Drama". Parallel with these sketches of a dramatic theory, the poet put on the stage successively: *The Rock* (1932), *Murder in the Cathedral* (1935), *The Family Reunion* (1943), *The Cocktail Party* (1948) and *The Confidential Clerk* (1952). In all these plays, Eliot's achievement gives valuable concrete support to his theory.

Whether or not we are susceptible to "poetic" values, we must agree with Eliot that the poetic form is the most appropriate, indeed the normal means of expression in the theatre. Eliot considers that a play ought always to be a poem. In his view Ibsen, Strindberg and Chekhov are true poets who feel hampered within the limits of prose. In contrast to these he cites Yeats and Hoffmansthal, who, at a time when prose drama predominated, kept alive the ancient and traditional affinity between drama and poetry.

We must undoubtedly admit that great dramatic poetry has the power to express a wider gamut of emotions than could any prose play, however noble. In poetic drama as in prose drama, the characters must be true to life, but they may also suggest something beyond life, transcending nature, and in this way open up vistas on to worlds unfamiliar to us. Thus they can express with mere words what, without verse, only music could convey. The listener may be unaware that the characters are "speaking verse", nevertheless he is subconsciously affected by the rhythm—as in the opening scenes of *Hamlet,* where the verse is transparent but communicates the magic of a frosty night, with men keeping watch, and the foreboding of an ominous action.

Taking Maeterlinck's plays as an example, Eliot considers that poetic drama in prose is, far more than verse drama, hampered and limited by the "poetic convention"[3] or at least by

[3] J. M. Synge's is a special case; his plays are set in a milieu which uses naturally poetic speech, and against an almost legendary background.

the conventional idea of what subject matter is "poetic".[4] As for the public, it must be taught to recognize and tolerate poetry in the mouths of characters wearing modern dress, living in modern homes, using cars and telephones.

Eliot seems influenced even more by the artistic theories of Yeats than by his theatrical work (although his last play, *Purgatory*, represents a genuine development and provides a model of its type.) "In poetical drama", Yeats wrote,

> ". . . there is, it is held, an antithesis between character and lyric poetry, for lyric poetry—however much it move you when read out of a book—can, as these critics think, but encumber the action. Yet when we go back a few centuries and enter the great periods of drama, character grows less and sometimes disappears, and there is much lyric feeling, and at times a lyric measure will be wrought into the dialogue, a flowing measure that had well befitted music, or that more lumbering one of the sonnet. Suddenly it strikes us that character is continuously present in comedy alone, and that there is much tragedy, that of Corneille, that of Racine, that of Greece and Rome, where its place is taken by passions and motives, one person being jealous, another full of love or remorse or pride or anger. In writers of tragi-comedy (and Shakespeare is always a writer of tragi-comedy) there is indeed character, but we notice that it is in the moments of comedy that character is defined, in Hamlet's gaiety, let us say; while amid the great moments, when Timon orders his tomb, when Hamlet cries to Horatio, 'Absent thee from felicity awhile', when Antony names 'Of many thousand kisses the poor last', all is lyricism, unmixed passion, 'the integrity of fire'."[5]

Besides Yeats and Hoffmansthal, Eliot might have instanced many other precursors of his venture. Claudel wrote poetic dramas whose action takes place in our own time and where characters in dinner jackets express themselves in poetry. . . Eliot might perhaps reply that Claudel's verse is rhythmic prose rather than verse in the true sense of the word. In England,

[4] Eliot has praised the dramatic gifts of Rostand in *Cyrano de Bergerac.*
[5] W. B. Yeats, "The Tragic Theatre", *Essays and Introductions,* p. 240.

fifty years before Eliot, Gerard Manley Hopkins had approached the problems of poetic drama with attitudes closely akin to those of the author of *Murder in the Cathedral.* But his work was not published until 1919, and then in incomplete form; it is therefore most unlikely that when Eliot started to write *The Rock* he had ever seen the sketches for *Saint Winifred,* a tragedy with choruses.[6]

A journalist once questioned Eliot about the part played by the supernatural element in his plays. The poet replied that he sought to *dépayser* his audience, to surround them with an unfamiliar atmosphere, as the only means of carrying them with him and inducing total participation. The audience must forget itself, so that the poetry it hears and sees becomes more real than its own reality. And when asked whether, when writing, he always had his prospective audience in mind, he replied with a smile that he did not think, while he was working, of those who would listen to his play; they formed part of the play itself, and it was in that capacity that he concerned himself with them, as he did with all the characters who could give his drama its meaning and its full intensity.[7]

We can apply to Eliot's plays what has been said of Shakespeare's—they should be interpreted not as disguised confessions or romantic fictions, but as theatrical compositions, poetic in character. Deeply imbued with the spirit of the Elizabethan drama, to which he has devoted some of his best essays, Eliot seeks, like Marlowe, Kyd and Webster, not to copy his characters from those of everyday life, but rather to transport us to unfamiliar regions. He is preoccupied above all with poetic causality, the chain of cause and effect, uniting episodes, peripateia and tableaux by mysterious laws whose "magical logic" is more akin to a dream than to the waking world. We may consider each of his plays, like those of Shakespeare, as "an extended metaphor, by means of which the original vision is projected in forms which correspond roughly to reality, and

[6] Since *The Rock* many plays in verse by W. H. Auden, Christopher Fry, etc. have been successfully performed in England and the U.S.A.

[7] Interview published in French.

conform to it more or less exactly according to the requirements of its nature. . ." so that the characters, all things considered, "are not human at all, but are the pure symbols of a poetic vision"[8] The fruitfulness of this principle of composition lies in the fact that every structural detail has its functional, architechtonic value, remaining closely linked with the other elements in the living, complex unity of the whole.[9]

The Rock, Eliot's first theatrical essay, is not a pageant in the usual sense of the word. It is not a string of historical tableaux; its intention is not merely to remind the audience that churches have been built at various times in the past, but to emphasize the needs of the present. In the first act, we see workers in the process of building a chapel—they are interrupted by a group of the unemployed. The value of this sketch, which resembles the mystery plays performed by medieval guilds, lies in the beauty of the antiphonal choruses intoned by workers and unemployed, and in the Biblical accent of the scenes which evoke Nehemiah's building of the Second Temple or the Rock on which Christ founded his Church :

> "The Eagle soars in the summit of Heaven,
> The Hunter with his dogs pursues his circuit.
> O perpetual revolution of configured stars,
> O perpetual recurrence of determined seasons,
> O world of spring and autumn, birth and dying !"

Despite its medieval and Christian theme, *Murder in the Cathedral* is closer to Greek tragedy than to Shakespeare's history plays or to Romantic drama.[10] Eliot however deliberately avoided Greek tragedy as a model, basing himself rather on the alliterative, assonanced and occasionally rhymed verse of *Everyman.* The mysteries of Grace and Predestination take the place of the Fates of Classical antiquity, and we might say that the

[8] G. Wilson Knight and H. Fluchère, *Présentation de Shakespeare, dramaturge élizabéthain.* Cahiers du Sud. (In French.)

[9] Note the cunning and deliberate mingling of prose and verse in Shakespeare's plays (e.g. the Porter scene in *Macbeth*).

[10] Such as Tennyson's *Thomas Becket.*

principal protagonist, together with the martyred Archbishop, is the Chorus. The play opens on December 2nd 1170, in front of Canterbury Cathedral, close to the porch where the Chorus, composed of the old women of the city, are lamenting as they await the return of Thomas Becket. During the prelate's exile, the common people have enjoyed if not security, at any rate a kind of apathy under oppression. But now these good gossips feel that *something is going to happen.* A herald announces the Archbishop's return; a priest vainly urges the poor old women to welcome the exile; they persist in their lamentations. We share their anxiety. (One recalls the Chorus in Aeschylus's *Persae,* awaiting the return of Xerxes to the palace of Suza). Thomas appears; and he exclaims:

> "Peace. And let them be, in their exaltation.
> They speak better than they know, and beyond your understanding.
> They know and do not know, what it is to act or suffer.
> They know and do not know, that acting is suffering
> And suffering is action. Neither does the actor suffer
> Nor the patient act. But both are fixed
> In an eternal action, an eternal patience
> To which all must consent that it may be willed
> And which all must suffer that they may will it,
> That the pattern may subsist, for the pattern is the action.
> And the suffering, that the wheel may turn and still
> Be forever still."

Thomas is not unaware of his people's "great fear"; he absolves them, because he shares it. Left alone, Thomas is visited by four mysterious strangers; these are the Tempters. The first reminds him of the "good times" when "gay Tom Becket of London", Chancellor of the Kingdom, enjoyed the King's favour, the time of pleasure parties on the Thames:

> "laughter and appleblossom floating on the water,
> "Singing at nightfall, whispering in chambers"

Those days have fled; the call of the past is not strong enough to beguile him.

The second Tempter whispers to Becket that

> "Power obtained grows to glory
> Life lasting, a permanent possession."

He replies: "To the man of God what gladness?" And then:

> "I *was* the King, his arm, his better reason.
> But what was once exaltation
> Would now be only mean descent."

The third voice—unexpected and yet foreseen by Thomas—is the voice of his caste: what is the use of trying to conciliate the King? "Blind assertion in isolation" is even more futile. He should ally himself with the Norman barons against a treacherous prince. The Archbishop rejects the tempter thus:

> "Shall I who ruled like an eagle over doves
> Now take the shape of a wolf among wolves?"

The fourth tempter makes the most subtle, because the most intimate, appeal. He has no name. Thomas has never seen him before. He personifies the desire for martyrdom, in so far as it is tainted with vain glory.

> "What earthly glory, of king or emperor,
> "What earthly pride, that is not poverty
> Compared with richness of heavenly grandeur?"

Thomas asks:

> "Who are you, tempting with my own desires?
> Others have come, temporal tempters,
> With pleasure and power at palpable price.
> What do you offer? what do you ask? . . .
> Others offered real goods, worthless
> But real. You only offer
> Dreams to damnation."

Thomas takes refuge in prayer, and emerges stronger, obedient to God's will, and intent on the salvation to be attained through his ordeal. Thus *Murder in the Cathedral* shows the resistance of the spiritual power, threatened by the intrusion of secular forces, while Becket, defenceless save for his faith, represents the interests of the Universal Church, which are those of all mankind.

An Interlude separates the first and second acts. It is Christmas morning, 1170. Next day will be the Feast of Stephen, the first martyr. Thomas goes up into the pulpit and preaches a sermon which constitutes a *credo*. (The text is in prose):

> "Is it an accident, do you think, that the day of the first martyr follows immediately the day of the birth of Christ?"

The time has now come for all things to be fulfilled. Following the order of Henry Plantagenet, four knights—or rather four mercenaries—burst sacrilegiously into the holy place, cynically listing the "crimes" committed by this just man; they threaten him and order him to leave his church and his flock. Thomas denies the misdeeds with which he is charged, and declares that only Rome has the right to judge him. While the King's confederates confer, the Chorus utter "subtle forebodings".

Then the hired assassins rush upon Thomas, stabbing him to death. The Chorus of housewives, now turned into avenging furies, speak mighty prophetic words:

> "Clear the air! clean the sky! wash the wind! take stone from stone and wash them . . .
> It is not we alone, it is not the house, it is not the city that is defiled,
> But the world that is wholly foul . . ."

The play might well have ended with this chorus. But it does not. In fact Eliot, changing the whole register and tone of the poem, gives us (in prose, this time) the speeches of the four murderers in self-defence. (Is there not here an ironic echo of the last scene in *Saint Joan,* where Shaw indulges in some irreverent interpretations of history?[11]) This scene is imbued with typically English humour. And then the chorus, transfigured, drives

[11] "I may, for aught I know, have been slightly under the influence of *St Joan.*" (Selected Prose, p. 79).

from our minds all these sophistries and specious arguments, with its hymn of praise and thanksgiving. There is a fine symmetry in the design, as in a medieval triptych: Thomas preaching in the centre, on the left the people acclaiming him in the Cathedral porch, and on the right his murder. Below, the four tempters and the four murderers.

THE FAMILY REUNION

After *Murder in the Cathedral*—and perhaps in reaction against the medieval style of that play, whose merit was, to use his own term, only negative—Eliot embarked on the first of a series of modern plays in verse, in which contemporary characters revive the Classical themes of antiquity.[12] His setting is a country house belonging to people of "good society"; and he shows these people's everyday life in all its irritating falseness and artificiality, due to the constant ambiguity and ceaseless misunderstandings of their social relationships, as well as to the confusion and instability of the personal relations between lovers or spouses. I know of no other instance where the role of *irony* in the theatrical illusion is expressed with such subtlety and caustic wit: a symbol of all these puerile adults "condemned to life" and searching, amidst tears and laughter, for their lost innocence.

Like his compatriot and contemporary O'Neill,[13] Eliot has always been attracted by the Oresteia, the tragedy of the Atrides. Both of them transposed it into a contemporary setting: O'Neill chose the War of Secession, Eliot the present day. The argument of this play—which Eliot later judged too harshly—runs as follows:

A young English peer, Harry, Lord Monchensey,[14] returns to his ancestral home, Wishwood. In the meanwhile his wife has died; she disappeared from the deck of a steamer during a

[12] Contrariwise, Giraudoux, Anouilh, Sartre. etc., make the heroes of Greek tragedy speak in modern colloquial idiom.

[13] Both were born in the United States in 1888.

[14] Eliot may have found this name in Browning's *In Bellum,* but Monchensey suggests Chauncy, his mother's maiden name.

crossing. Harry no longer knows whether he pushed her overboard or whether he merely wanted to do so. Perhaps she committed suicide? Perhaps she fell overboard because she was drunk? Harry is about to face a regular *conseil de famille:* his mother, his aunts, his uncles, a young cousin. He learns that his Aunt Agatha had been in love with her brother-in-law, Lord Monchensey; and that this brother-in-law, Harry's own father, had wanted to kill his wife. Harry has a dark heredity; perhaps he was impelled to fulfil his father's desire? Through the dining-room window he has a vision of the avenging Eumenides. He can no longer live in such a place; he decides to go away: but where?

"... that is still unsettled.
I have not yet had the precise directions.
Where does one go from a world of insanity?
Somewhere on the other side of despair
To the worship in the desert, the thirst and deprivation,
A stony sanctuary and a primitive altar ..."

Henceforth, as his aunt Agatha declares:

"Here the danger, here the death, here, not elsewhere;
Elsewhere no doubt is agony, renunciation,
But birth and life. Harry has crossed the frontier
Beyond which safety and danger have a different meaning ..."

* *

In his essay on "Poetry and Drama",[15] Eliot judges *The Family Reunion* somewhat harshly. He accuses himself of taking up "far too much of the strictly limited time allowed to a dramatist in presenting a situation"; he therefore had not enough time to develop the action, which in any case he considers not sufficiently substantial. On the whole, he is satisfied with the first act, apart from its being "far too long". When the curtain rises, "the audience is expecting, as it has a right to expect, that something is going to happen. Instead, it finds itself treated to a further exploration of the background". And in the

[15] *Selected Prose,* p. 67.

second act, after allowing the audience's attention to wander, "the conclusion comes so abruptly that we are, after all, unready for it." In addition, Eliot considers that "the deepest flaw of all was a failure of adjustment between the Greek story and the modern situation"; he should either "have stuck closer to Aeschylus or else taken a great deal more liberty with his myth." The Eumenides, the Furies, seem here out of place. Eliot expresses the wish that they should in future "be understood to be visible only to certain of my characters and not to the audience". Moreover, Eliot considers that he has failed to reconcile the two situations, the tragedy of the mother and the salvation of the son. (He even adds that the son now strikes him as an insufferable prig). Eliot also criticises his own use of lyrical interludes which, even more than the choruses, hold up the action and serve merely as *hors d'oeuvre*. But despite the severity of the author's judgment, *The Family Reunion* is undeniably an impressive work.

THE COCKTAIL PARTY

Fifteen years after *Murder in the Cathedral,* twelve years after *The Family Reunion,* Eliot returned to drama, with a tone and a theme *apparently* less austere. From now on, there are no more choruses or ghosts.

The Cocktail Party, written for the 1950 Edinburgh Festival, seems at first sight to be only a comedy, in which the audience is free to imagine that it understands what is taking place on the stage; the true theme of the play, however, lies elsewhere. We are confronted at the outset with a quartet of beings each of whom is desperately alone. When the curtain rises, Edward Chamberlayne, lover of the unresponsive Celia Copplestone, has just been deserted by his wife Lavinia. He is therefore obliged to act as sole host at the cocktail party, where we meet young Peter Quilpe, Lavinia's lover but also in love with Celia. Among the other guests are two colourful characters who, though they appear to play the role of mere confidants, have in fact a far from secondary significance. These ministering angels, indiscreet and persistent, are called Alex and Julia. They fulfil their mission with superb tactlessness; they are, as we shall see, secret messengers of a mysterious master.

In this strange play the poet, rejecting a form of speech that has become mere jargon, distorted and debased by men, has not merely sought to invent an idiom; he has applied a mute to his instrument, and at first produces only harsh, discordant notes recalling the satiric tone of *Prufrock* or *Sweeney's* cruelly caustic irony... Is this a joke at our expense? As Alfred Simon[16] has rightly stressed, the first act, "with its liveliness and its surprises, seems like the ghostly analysis of some comedy by Labiche or Feydeau, making pointless any search for an ideal explanation. It is indeed a violent assault on highmindedness; and the ambiguity of the characters' behaviour is an ironic expression of quintessential theatricality."

We feel here that "real life is absent"—absent, that is, until the intrusion of the mysterious stranger reintroduces a sense of otherworldliness among these weak, degenerate and incoherent beings. It is a real stroke of genius to bring into this lively, futile shadow-play the terrible "unspoken Word, the Word unheard", the key word to every soul. And yet even here we feel, as in *Ash Wednesday* and the *Quartets,* "the end is in the beginning, the beginning in the end." "Will these bones live?" There is the whole question. These are indeed "simple souls"; each of them

> "moving between the legs of tables and of chairs,
> Rising or falling, grasping at kisses and toys . . ."[17]

But here, too, we perceive the "heavy burden of the growing soul".

The word "cocktail" describes a mixture of alcoholic drinks as strange and variegated as a cock's tail,[18] and just such a mixture is provided by the reunion (by no means a family one) of the seven protagonists, whether they are patients (Edward, Lavinia, Peter and Celia) or agents (the psychiatrist and his

[16] *Esprit,* July 1954.
[17] cf. *Animula.*
[18] According to Bevan, Eliot detests cocktails and cocktail parties.

satellites). For among all these restless, petty souls, writhing like fishes caught in a net, there is one great soul, unconscious of itself, which must be brought to life by the Leader of the Game, like Herakles the guest of Admetus in Euripedes' Alcestis. For it was in fact from this Greek tragedy that Eliot drew his inspiration. (No single critic perceived this, much to the author's amusement).

The Cocktail Party is as much a comedy of manners as a psychological drama, as much a *pièce à thèse* as a satire of high society, as much a mystery place as a farce. Possibly it is a fable. Beneath a veil of humour, typically British and very contemporary, lies concealed a tragi-comedy for which any large city, in any decadent, disillusioned age might provide an apt setting. But it is more akin to Aristophanes and to Euripides than to Aeschylus. . . A stranger, a mysterious guest, bearing the name of Sir Henry Harcourt-Reilly, the distinguished psychiatrist, takes upon himself the godlike task of revealing to these puppets their true nature, hitherto stifled by conventionality, by social graces or individual obsessions; in a word, their secret desires and aspirations, their purpose in life, their vocation or dedication. The intricacies of the plot—as complex as those of Marivaux, Congreve or Plautus—are not really significant. With the help of his acolytes, Alex and Julia (who, under the disguise of their absurd mannerisms, conceal their role of protective genii, indeed of guardian angels), Sir Henry succeeds in reconciling Edward and his wife Lavinia, who were supremely well matched despite their mutual indifference, or indeed precisely because of this shared aridity. . . As for Celia, she is cast in a different mould. By the end of the story we learn that this pale, frustrated young woman, this Christian Alcestis, had a martyr's vocation; and there is something fearful in this conjunction of innocence with death deliberately sought. We are now as remote from the mood of farce as from that of sentimental comedy. Lavinia's flight reveals the flimsy, shallow nature of this small world of futile, wealthy bourgeois. Beneath their forced animation and their sparkling inanity, they are poor frightened creatures trying to hide profound anxiety. All their quips and grimaces, their hectic chatter, cannot conceal the fact that *something else* is at stake. Under superficial comedy—a game of blind man's buff or general post—lies some horrible silence. Each of the characters has come to realise that he is alone—that every one of us, whatever he may do, is utterly alone. Then the dance starts up again, in a different vein; for with Sir Henry, the strange, new and unknown element intrudes; and the discordant quartet becomes a septet, the quadrille becomes a ritual dance presided over, from near or from far, by the great magician and his acolytes. Through the incantatory libation of the "three" (an obscure allusion here to three other tutelary figures) the farce has become a fable in dialogue, a hidden mystery, in which the bitter clash of selfish desires gives way before the patience of those who are journeying towards "the peace that passeth all understanding".

Stanislas Fumet has noted an original feature distinguishing Eliot from Claudel, namely that in this work the protective spirits always expect the beings under their care to act *of their own free will,* not under the influence of some compelling love, like Prouhèze in *Le Soulier de Satin,* urged on by her Angel. This trivial world is suddenly absorbed into the world of light! Fumet compares Eliot's Sir Henry with Chesterton's huge "Sunday" in *The man who was Thursday,* and observes that Eliot is "one of that line of English poets and novelists who have renewed contact with God by way of other-worldly humour." Through the poet's magic power, humour, music and a spiritual vision are fused. There is no denying the fact that his play is admirable theatre, and upon analysis there also emerges a kind of musical pattern, which supplements the force of the dramatic action with which it is subconsciously fused, exciting or allaying our emotions. As in Shakespeare, the transitions obey the laws both of music and of dramatic action. Thus we might trace—as Eliot did in *Hamlet*—a twofold plot, unfolding simultaneously on the dramatic and musical levels. In this way we might be able to analyze the unconscious effect that the poetic language has upon us, and not only on lovers of poetry but also upon those who are interested only in the story of the play. (Indeed, we feel that Eliot, while writing this play, constantly bore in mind such people, who never open a book of verse). Whereas when writing his poems, he wants to hear the sound of his own voice, since he is speaking in his own name (and "communication" is then of secondary importance) here, in a play, he is deliberately writing verse for other voices, verse which will arouse an immediate response from an unknown audience and which will be spoken by unknown actors. He must therefore obey the laws of dramatic propriety.

THE CONFIDENTIAL CLERK

Thus, after two centuries of neglect,[19] the verse play or dramatic poem seems likely to come into favour in England again, thanks largely to Eliot's recent experiments. Each successive play gives stronger evidence of his mastery. After the achievement of *The Cocktail Party* comes that of *The Confidential Clerk*. In both these works, the poet has tackled the most apparently unpromising material: a contemporary story involving men and women like those we all know, dressed in the fashion of today, facing the problems, difficulties and misunderstandings that constantly confront us all. Eliot seems to borrow some devices from Congreve, but he inverts them, using them in reverse with a moral end in view. From Congreve to Shaw, by way of Wycherley, Sheridan, Dickens and Wilde, English comedy had been largely an entertainment, a game, where the characters seem to be "their own puppets". Laughter had the flimsiest basis; the comic element was carried to the point of absurdity. The characters had a carefree impertinence, the dialogue was cut-and-thrust repartee.

To summarize the plot of this new play: Sir Claude Mulhammer, a well-to-do financier, despite a number of youthful affairs, has always chiefly loved his speculations on the Stock Exchange. . . As he grows old, he feels rather lonely, since he has no children by his wife, Lady Elizabeth, an eccentric

[19] The poems in dialogue by Tennyson, Browning and Swinburne scarcely count as plays. Beddoes' dramas are certainly superior. Otway's *Venice Preserved* survives, and possibly Shelley's *Cenci*.

grande dame. When the curtain rises, Sir Claude is about to appoint a successor for his private secretary, the faithful Eggerson, who is retiring. The new candidate for the post, Colby Simpkins, a frail dreamer, would appear to be the illegitimate son of Sir Claude. Mulhammer divulges his secret to Eggerson, confessing his wish to see Lady Elizabeth become so infatuated with Colby that she will adopt him legally. Everything happens according to plan; in fact things go further than he has anticipated; the good lady believes Colby to be her own child, the result of a youthful indiscretion before her marriage. Meanwhile Sir Claude makes certain admissions to his new secretary, so thinly veiled that Colbly believes himself to be in fact his employer's son. Then things become more complicated. An impulsive girl falls in love with Colby—she is in fact the ward and the illegitimate daughter of Sir Claude; she confesses this to the young man, and is amazed to see him grow more distant towards her, believing himself to be her brother and yet unable to betray his secret.

Lucasta therefore resigns herself to marrying another protégé of Sir Claude's, Barnabas Kaghan (always known as "B", his Christian name being considered vulgar), a self-seeking young man whom Lady Elizabeth cannot abide. Now the action takes place in Colby's rooms. There appears on the scene one Mrs Guzzard, Colby's old nurse, to whom Lady Elizabeth had entrusted her infant. And was this Colby? Not at all; the noble lady's son is none other than that vulgarian Barnabas Kaghan. Nor is Colby, as it turns out, Sir Colby's son; his parents were Mrs Guzzard and a penniless musician. The old nurse confesses that in the hope of winning the financier's favours for her son she had substituted him for the child that her own sister had borne to Mulhammer, who in fact did not live. Simpkins, who had no taste for high life, at last feels himself free to pursue his vocation as organist. He may also, eventually, become a priest. Sir Claude, bereft of a son, turns to Lucasta, for whom he suddenly feels an unexpected affection.[20]

[20] The play is inspired by Euripides' *Ion,* where Creusa and Xanthos each think Ion is their son.

All this is told with delicacy and discretion. It would be absurd to liken this play, as certain critics have done, to an entertainment like *The Importance of Being Earnest*. In this close-knit, disciplined and vigorous "diversion", there is no line of dialogue, however trivial it may seem, that does not fulfil some dramatic necessity. It is light and sparkling, and yet poignant, like a Mozart quartet or a sketch by Toulouse-Lautrec. Here is nothing excessive. Underlying the ironical imbroglio there lies the grief of all those who suffer loneliness and grope in the darkness for someone to love. For the poet, here, seems to be leading us by way of music to some serene reconciliation.

As another poet, Claudel, has put it, faith gives a symbolic quality to the actions presented in the drama: "Nothing takes place in isolation any more, but in relation to a higher reality, to the great drama of the Creation and of Salvation which acts as a basis and on which this is a sort of individual commentary, a parable in action." Eliot's plays, like those of Calderon and Claudel, are evidence that drama and religion can prove mutually enriching.

THE ELDER STATESMAN

This latest play of Eliot's was performed at the 1958 Edinburgh Festival and was very well received by audiences and critics. In the *Elder Statesman* some of the themes of *Oedipus at Colonnus* are transposed into a modern setting and modern dress, but this work is both less ambitious than *The Cocktail Party* and less informal than *The Confidential Clerk*. The hero, Lord Claverton, is an old statesman who has retired from public life into a nursing home in the country, under the loving and watchful care of his daughter. He is nevertheless pursued, even in this peaceful retreat, by the rancour and the threats of two sinister figures from his past. One is a former Oxford student, who has lived in the Argentine and become a dangerous swindler, and who ceaselessly reminds him of a dark incident in his youth: he had driven over the body of a man lying on the road, and had not stopped to help him. The other figure is a music hall actress whom he had once seduced and to whom he has had to pay large sums of money to avoid blackmail. These two intriguers manage to involve in their schemes Claverton's rebellious son. But in vain, for the old statesman, by confessing his sins to his daughter, has learnt how to win pardon, compassion and true humility by achieving self-awareness. Now freed from the ghosts of his past as well as from the lies and illusions for which he has lived so long, Lord Claverton can die in peace . . . And we see him sitting under the shade of an old oak-tree, mysteriously passing away in the evening calm.

Several critics have attributed the atmosphere of optimism and occasional tenderness that reigns in this latest work to the poet's recent marriage with his young and charming secretary, Miss Valerie Fletcher.

6. *Aesthetics and Criticism*

Culture and Christianity

GOETHE ONCE observed that the work of a poet who relied entirely on his own inner resources would be poor indeed. Eliot is of the same opinion. He writes: "No poet, no artist of any art has his complete meaning alone. His significance, his appreciation is the appreciation of his relation to the dead poets and artist. You cannot value him alone; you must set him, for contrast and comparison, among the dead. I mean this as a principle of aesthetic, not merely historical, criticism."[1]

In various essays[2] and above all in the study which made him famous, "Tradition and the Individual Talent", Eliot links the life and particular contribution of each artist with the universal life of the human race; he affirms the continuity of the ages, and suggests a kind of "reversibility" of influences which gives to the creative force of genius a unity that is almost supernatural, and that leads to an end.

"What happens when a new work of art is created is something that happens simultaneously to all the works of art which preceded it. The existing monuments form an ideal order among themselves, which is modified by the introduction of the new (the really new) work of art among them. The existing order is complete before the new work arrives; for order to persist after the supervention of novelty, the *whole* existing order must be, if ever so slightly, altered; and so the relations, proportions, values of each work of art towards the whole are readjusted;

[1] "Tradition and the Individual Talent", *The Egoist,* October 1919, and *Selected Essays,* Faber, 1934. p. 15.

[2] *The Sacred Wood, Selected Essays, For Lancelot Andrewes,* etc.

and this is conformity between the old and the new. Whoever has approved this idea of order, of the form of European, of English literature, will not find it preposterous that the past should be altered by the present as much as the present is directed by the past. And the poet who is aware of this will be aware of great difficulties and responsibilities."[3]

Thus Eliot requires, to form the poet's environment, "an easy commerce of the old and the new". And what is, in fact, the external authority to which Eliot considers a writer should submit himself and obey? "Between the true artists of any time there is, I believe, an unconscious community. . .[4] Whenever we cling to an old tradition or attempt to reestablish one, "we are always in danger of confusing the vital and the unessential, the real and the sentimental. Our second danger is to associate tradition with the immovable; to think of it as something hostile to all change; to aim to return to some previous condition which we imagine as having been capable of preservation in perpetuity, instead of aiming to stimulate the life which produced that condition in its time."[5]

Thus in Eliot's work the presence of the past attains tremendous and almost symbolic force. Like Malraux, Eliot contrasts true creation, which strives for the unattainable, with convention, which is content to imitate former models. Aware that our age is in search of its own consciousness, he questions "all the consciousnesses of the past". "We dwell with satisfaction upon the poet's difference from his predecessors, especially his immediate predecessors; we endeavour to find something that can be isolated in order to be enjoyed. Whereas if we approach a poet without this prejudice we shall often find that not only the best but the most individual parts of his work may be those in which the dead poets, his ancestors, assert their immortality most vigorously."[6]

The really great poet is not the one who merely revives a

[3] "Tradition and the Individual Talent", *Selected Essays,* pp. 15 and 23. *The Sacred Wood.*

[4] *Selected Essays,* p. 24.

[5] *After Strange Gods,* 1954.

[6] *Selected Essays,* p. 14.

tradition which has fallen into disuse, but the one who is able to join together as many as possible of the disconnected branches of tradition. Eliot emphasizes that tradition is not inherited, that it can only be acquired "by great labour". "It involves in the first place the historical sense, which we may call nearly indispensable to anyone who would continue to be a poet beyond his twenty-fifth year; and the historical sense compels a man to write not merely with his own generation in his bones, but with a feeling that the whole of the literature of Europe from Homer and within it the whole of the literature of his own country has a simultaneous existence and composes a simultaneous order . . . it is . . . what makes a writer most acutely conscious of his place in time, of his contemporaneity."[7]

It is this historical sense which makes Eliot a Classical writer and a humanist.

The disciplines to which Eliot willingly submits are normally intolerable to the individualistic Anglo-Saxon temperament, which tends to condemn reticence in poetry, seeking between the lines for traces of autobiographical confession. But art can only be achieved when the artist has ceased to take an interest in his own feelings and experiences. "It is not in his personal emotions . . . that the poet is in any way remarkable or interesting. . . The business of the poet is . . . to transmute his personal and private agonies into something rich and strange, something universal and impersonal."[8]

For Eliot as for Baudelaire. "rhetoric and prosody are not arbitrarily invented tyrannies, but a collection of rules demanded by the very organization of the mind. Nor have prosody or rhetoric ever prevented originality from making itself clearly felt. The poet owes it to himself to create his own routine." Eliot would agree with Hegel that "though artistic forms have their origin in the *idea* which they express, this in its turn is truly an idea only when it is realised in these forms." In his view an idea, in the highest sense of the word, can be expressed only by a symbol. He protests against those who see

[7] "Tradition and the Individual Talent," *Selected Essays.*
[8] ibid.

in "beauty" nothing but an arbitrary source of sensual satisfaction, empirical and subjective, whereas aesthetic judgment is the affirmation of a universally communicable pleasure.

"There is a great deal, in the writing of poetry, which must be conscious and deliberate. In fact the bad poet is usually unconscious where he ought to be conscious, and conscious where he ought to be unconscious. Both errors tend to make him 'personal'. Poetry is not a turning loose of emotion, but an escape from emotion; it is not the expression of personality, but an escape from personality. But of course, only those who have personality and emotions know what it means to want to escape from these things."[9]

In order to clarify his position and the relation of this process of depersonalization to traditional poetry, Eliot compares the role of the individual poet to that of a catalyst. In chemical catalysis the combination of two gases takes place only in the presence of a filament of platinum; "nevertheless the newly-formed acid contains no trace of platinum, and the platinum itself is apparently unaffected. . . The mind of the poet is the shred of platinum. It may partly or exclusively operate upon the experience of the man himself; but the more perfect the artist, the more completely separate in him will be the man who suffers and the mind which creates; the more perfectly will the mind digest and transmute the passions which are its material."[10]

Ramon Fernandez[11] has emphasized that Eliot's great merit was that, while surveying the "middle and temperate regions" of literature, he defined the "summits of classicism, namely the analysis of Aristotle and the vision of Dante," which are rightly seen as "the eternal forms of criticism and poetry." For Eliot, the only way to express an emotion in artistic form is to find an "objective correlative", in other words a set of objects, a situation, a sequence of events which constitute the formula for that particular emotion. in such a way that, when the ex-

[9] ibid. [10] ibid.
[11] R. Fernandez, "Le Classicisme de T. S. Eliot", *Messages* I, p. 218.

ternal factors which must lead to a sensory experience are given, the emotion is immediately evoked."[12]

This attitude causes Eliot to judge *Hamlet* with particular severity, since the emotion in the play is in excess of the facts which arouse it. In the *Divine Comedy,* on the other hand, Eliot finds "a strict correspondence between the expression and what is expressed." Far from filtering Dante's lyricism and rejecting the doctrinal framework of the poem, he finds the philosophy "essential to the structure and the structure to the beauty of the poem's parts." The case of Blake is the counterpart to that of Dante. "Blake was endowed with a capacity for considerable understanding of human nature, with a remarkable and original sense of language and the music of language, and a gift of hallucinated vision. What his genius required, and what it sadly lacked, was a framework of accepted and traditional ideas which would have prevented him from indulging in a philosophy of his own, and concentrated his attention upon the problems of the poet. Confusion of thought, emotion and vision is what we find in such a work as *Also Sprach Zarathustra;* it is eminently not a Latin virtue. The concentration resulting from a framework of mythology and theology and philosophy is one of the reasons why Dante is a classic, and Blake only a poet of genius."[13]

While admiring Eliot's "courage and fine precision" Fernandez emphasizes the dangerous aspect of a doctrine which nevertheless corresponded to his own secret preferences. Without confusing (as so many others have done) Eliot's objectivism with the positivism of Taine or Gourmont, Fernandez has shown that "if we are no longer guided by an impelling immediate pleasure . . . we may well be influenced exclusively by an ideal image", whereas it should be recognized that art is "relative to the age, to the social context, to the degree of clarity in thought, and that a confused masterpiece represents a revealing attempt to break away from the confusion." In short, the author of *Messages* concludes, there must needs be

[12] "Hamlet and his Problems", *The Sacred Wood,* p. 92.
[13] "Blake", *The Sacred Wood,* p. 143.

periods of achievement and periods of preparation and of birth.

Criticism and Poetry

Criticism, Eliot declares, endeavours either to discover what poetry is, what is its use, what desires it satisfies, why it is written, read or recited, or else, these things being assumed to be known consciously or unconsciously, to consider poetry in itself. Baudelaire asserted that "all great poets naturally and inevitably become critics. . ." and even said: "I am sorry for those poets who are guided by instinct alone; I believe them to be incomplete. It would be astonishing if a critic became a poet, and it is impossible for a poet not to contain within himself a critic. The reader will not be surprised, therefore, if I consider the poet as the best of all critics."[14] Eliot goes even further than this. Like Proust, he has no hesitation in likening the poet's work to that of the scientist. Speaking of the contribution of the French Symbolists, he declares that it would be as absurd for a poet to ignore the work of his predecessors as for a biologist to repeat the experiments of Mendel; that the French poets in question had made discoveries in poetry which we no longer had the right to ignore.[15]

Eliot has clearly pointed out that criticism of poetry moves between two extremes; "On the one hand the critic may busy himself so much with the implications of a poem, or of one poet's work—implications moral, social, religious or other—that the poetry becomes hardly more than a text for a discourse. Such is the tendency of the moralizing critics of the nineteenth century, to which Landor makes a notable exception. Or if you stick too closely to the "poetry" and adopt no attitude towards what the poet has to say, you will tend to evacuate it of all significance."[16]

Criticizing romanticism, Eliot attacks first and foremost the primacy of the emotional life. He seeks to dissipate the fog of

[14] *L'Art Romantique,* p. 219.
[15] *The Egoist,* June-July 1918.
[16] *The Use of Poetry,* p. 64.

feeling which distracts and confuses the reader. Very early on, the serious nature of his ambitions was to lead Eliot to reflect upon the design and structure of the poetic work he intended to create. He wanted this work to be the expression of his own time. For this poet, who professed adherence to the soundest traditions of the past, was in no way an anachronistic bard; by his themes as much as by his technique, he was to show himself an innovator, a rebel; and one might say of his poems, from *Prufrock* to *The Waste Land,* what Hugo said of Balzac's novels: that "the whole of our contemporary civilization can be seen in motion there, with something terrifying and terrified mingled with reality." Eliot was soon to discover that even in a world which has lost its state of integration and its vitality, authentic poetry can attain its full stature provided (as Maritain has said) the poet is aware of certain extremely simple but basic *presences,* "existential certainties ensured by the universe of thought which constitutes the vital environment for poetic intuition"; for instance, "the certainty that between man and the world there exists a kinship deeper than all material relationships. . ."

While maintaining the best traditions of the Classical heritage, Eliot discarded nothing of the conquests of Symbolism. He integrates these acquisitions into the twofold tradition of Graeco-Latin humanism and Anglo-Celtic lyricism. Few writers have undergone such disparate influences as he. While profoundly versed in Elizabethan literature, he is equally indebted to the Greeks, the Latins and even the Hindus. . . And the influence of Hebrew lyricism has nowhere been more marked than in the work of that poet whose ancestors, for generations, read and meditated and commented the Holy Scriptures. . . Eliot bears witness to this: "Our civilization comprehends great variety and complexity, and this variety and complexity, playing upon a refined sensibility, must produce various and complex results. The poet must become more and more comprehensive, more allusive, more indirect, in order to force, to dislocate, if necessary, language into his meaning."[17]

[17] *Selected Essays,* p. 289.

Eliot's art is essentially elliptical, and often, in his metaphors, the first term is suppressed, leaving the obscure, hidden analogy to be guessed at; the transsubstantiation is fully accomplished by the image. "Critics sometimes comment", he writes, "upon the sudden transitions and juxtapositions of modern poetry. . . Whether the transition is cogent or not is merely a question of whether the mind is *serré* or *délié,* whether the whole personality is involved. . ." And he concludes with these words, which might be applied to himself: "it is the unity of personality which gives an indissoluble unity to his variety of subject."[18]

Eliot's thought made a powerful impression on the younger generation. They feel, with Joubert, that "taste ought to be the literary conscience of the soul, and criticism the methodical application of this". Such indeed is the nature of Eliot's criticism, and from this it derives its influence. In his essay "The Use of Poetry and the Use of Criticism" (lectures given at Harvard in 1933), Eliot considered the problem of the relations between criticism and poetry.[19] When people ask the question: "What is poetry?" it often happens, he points out, that the person addressed answers on a wholly different point, for instance what purpose does poetry serve, what is its use? Eliot seems not to have tried to define poetry himself, perhaps because he considers it undefinable. On the other hand he shows us, with consistency and clarity, what critics at different periods have expected of poetry, and how their appreciation of the different poetic genres has varied.

Highly though he esteems the work of Mallarmé and that of Valéry, whose formulation of the doctrine of art for art's sake he finds superior to that of Pater and Wilde, Eliot protests against the paradox according to which, the work being no longer connected with any external object to which it might pay hommage, "the writer is led to consider himself as more

[18] ibid, p. 462.

[19] On these various points, Eliot's thought is strikingly akin to that of Proust. According to E. J. H. Greene, Eliot was impressed by the effectiveness of this critical method on reading *La Nouvelle Revue Française* in January 1920, and retained a lasting memory of it.

important than the work itself." There are, however, other aspects of Valéry's thought which could not fail to interest the author of *The Sacred Wood*. Eliot has stated that strange as it may seem, his intimacy with Valéry's poetry is largely due to his study of Valéry's writings about poetry; and that of all poets Valéry was the most completely lucid, or the closest to lucidity. Moreover, Eliot notes that he had frequently perceived that Valéry's analyses of the poetic process corresponded to his own on points of which he had only been obscurely aware.[20]

Eliot does not forget that "literary criticism should be completed by criticism from a definite ethical and theological standpoint. The "greatness" of literature cannot be determined solely by literary standards; though we must remember that whether it is literature or not can be determined only by literary standards."[21] Thus it is the subject and the mode of thought that determine the style. This leads Eliot to display a somewhat excessive severity towards the works of Hugo, Barrès and Peguy.

The Poet's Philosophy

Eliot has frequently deplored the difficulty experienced in ordinary life of maintaining the high level of those passions conducive to art and analysis.[22] He has therefore always striven to attain an ever greater integrity, both through the intensity of his vision and through his concern for exact expression. He makes an end to the conflict which, ever since Plato, had divided poets from philosophers, and praises good philosophical writing, whether that of Aristotle, Bradley, Richard de Saint-Victor or Bertrand Russell. He also appreciates the French moralists of the seventeeth century because of the honesty with which they face the data of the modern world. The unity of a work depends on the unity within the author's mind; and in our own day, in a complex and varied civilization, the author

[20] "Leçon de Paul Valéry" in *Valéry Vivant,* Cahiers du Sud.
[21] *Essays Ancient and Modern.* p. 93.
[22] "Beyle and Balzac", Athenaeum, May 30th 1919.

must become increasingly comprehensive, even at the cost of appearing difficult. Does this mean that the poet must become a metaphysician? Eliot had formerly rejected such a notion, asserting that a poet who was equally a metaphysician, such as Valéry's M. Teste, would be a monster, as inconceivable as a unicorn; that it was simpler for a poet to adopt another's philosophy, if necessary, than to create his own. Dante and Lucretius had done so; Lucretius indeed had passionately identified himself with the Epicurean system, finding therein something greater than himself.[23]

Recently, Eliot has returned to this vexed question. He inclines to think that we can give two different meanings to the expression "a poet's philosophy"; on the one hand, a "philosophy" which he has borrowed or which he has tried to construct himself in the *language of philosophy;* on the other, a philosophy which can only be expressed in *the language of poetry,* and this is in the truest sense the poet's original work. When, in order to understand Dante better, we study the metaphysics of Aristotle and St Thomas Aquinas, we enrich our knowledge of the original material of the poem; but the philosophy of Dante *qua* poet is something different from his philosophy *qua* disciple of the philosophers. If, for instance, when we consider certain philosophical passages in the *Purgatorio* we translate them in the terms of Aristotle's *De Anima,* we are astonished that the poet could have transformed into poetry such austere and refractory stuff. Eliot has asked himself the question: Must we consider poetry as a vehicle for the expression of our ideas, of our beliefs, of our emotions, of our observations and our experience, or must we consider these ideas, beliefs, emotions, observations and experience simply as the material from which a poem is made? And he replies by distinguishing first between the problem of the reader (who may be mistaken in his interpretation) and that of the poet, who may conceive one thing and realise another. The poet may make a fine poem with a minimum of strictly poetic means, or with an insignificant content; as an example of the first Eliot

[23] "Leçon de Paul Valéry", *Valéry Vivant,* Cahiers du Sud.

quotes the verse of St John of the Cross, and of the second, the songs of Shakespeare. Eliot includes himself in the first category: that of the poets who might have been philosophers (and we know that philosophy was his original vocation). It goes without saying that the value of the poem remains distinct from the importance of the ideas on which it is based. Moreover, beneath a philosophic structure, the poet may introduce a great deal of himself, up to the point where putting the maximum of one's being into a poem leads finally to the maximum of impersonality. He remains a poet because if the content of his poems is translated into abstract terms it is changed into something else, into something of less value. . . Eliot admits moreover that his own ideas, once they are set out in definitive order, surprise him as though they were someone else's. And the completed work is rarely what the author had in view when he first set to work; it is a long apprenticeship, where each attempt is a new departure, where "each adventure is a new beginning: a raid on the inarticulate". In fact (as he has himself insinuated when speaking of Donne, Poe or Mallarmé) Eliot uses metaphysical theories only in order to attain a more limited end: to refine and develop his faculty for feeling. His work is an expansion of his sensibility beyond the limits of the normal world.

After his long journey through the waste land, Eliot, reaching his haven, has settled there; he has taken for his own Maurras's confession of faith: "Sensibility, saved from itself and brought to order, has become a principle of perfection." In fact, it was only after long and painful groping that this poet deliberately adopted such rigorous doctrines. During a controversy with Middleton Murry, Eliot wrote that men can only live by submitting themselves to something outside themselves. When Murry suggested that they should obey an inner voice, Eliot replied that this inner voice sounds remarkably like the old principle "doing as one likes" and "breathes the eternal message of vanity, fear and lust."[24] It is however untrue to say, as some of his detractors[25] have done, that Eliot has

[24] "The Function of Criticism," *Selected Essays*, p. 27.
[25] For instance Carl Sandburg, Oliver Todd, R. H. Robbins.

become the poet of a reactionary bourgeoisie. Neither is he a Fascist or a follower of Maurras.[26] In an interview with a French paper, he has clarified his position. Despite his agreement on certain points with both Maurras and Maritain, he denies being a disciple of either. He is a "traditionalist" without the derogatory political nuance that the French attribute to the term; holding that not all of the past must be preserved, and that what is retained must be revivified, he considers himself a selective conservative *(un conservateur difficile)*; and claims that his conception of tradition as something constantly renewed, constantly moving, is a revolutionary one.

What must be said is that this poet of American birth is a humanist in the fullest sense of the term: the poetry of the Italian renaissance—that of Dante, Guinicelli and Cavalcanti—is as familiar to him as that of Elizabethan tragedy. He likes to point out that in order to remain a poet after one's twenty-fifth year one must possess not only a historic sense but a sense of the past, constantly present. If the poet of *Prufrock* has been able to renew himself so many times it is because he possesses unbounded curiosity. Eliot is no aesthete like Walter Pater. He cannot rest content with pure enjoyment; he has to transform his delight into knowledge. And for him, as for Baudelaire, aesthetic redemption only raises the religious problem more urgently. Eliot does not want to be classed among devotional or philosophical poets. This would limit his poetic field of vision. Yet no poetry deserves more than his the name of a *spiritual exercise*.

"The important fact about Baudelaire", he says, "is that he was essentially a Christian, born out of his time. . . And being the kind of Christian that he was, born when he was, he had to discover Christianity for himself. In this pursuit he was alone in the solitude which is known only to saints. To him the notion

[26] Eliot's aesthetic and social doctrines have undoubtedly been influenced by such works as Maurras' *L'Avenir de l'Intelligence,* Irving Babbitt's *Democracy and Leadership,* Sorel's *Réflexions sur la Violence,* T. E. Hulme's *Speculations,* Benda's *Belphégor* and Maritain's *Réflexions sur l'Intelligence.*

of Original Sin came spontaneously, and the need for prayer... And Baudelaire came to attain the greatest, the most difficult of the Christian virtues, the virtue of humility."[27]

It might be said that Eliot's purpose, like that of Dante, is "to rescue those who live in this life from their state of misery and lead them into a state of felicity"[28]. And his poetry has remained, if not an instrument of salvation, at least "an autonomous creation in which are reflected the wanderings of sinful humanity in pursuit of beatitude." It is doubtless from his master Alighieri that Eliot learnt the art of never wearying his reader by indoctrination. Thanks to what Maritain has called "the creative innocence of the poet" both these writers, the man of the Middle Ages and our own contemporary, succeed in creating living allegories as a vehicle for abstract ideas, uplifted and transfigured with poetic imagination. Thus the allegory becomes "visual melody" and gives us intuitive delight, so that we merely have to know that it has a meaning even though we do not understand it. "Reading the poem, you suspend both belief and disbelief."[29] And we never experience that feeling of uneasiness which certain other poets impose on us (Goethe, for example), the uneasiness of finding oneself in presence of a man who is trying to impose on one his own way of seeing. Eliot points out that Dante's "private belief becomes a different thing in becoming poetry."[30] It would be tempting to suggest that "this is truer of Dante than of any other philosophical poet." Eliot adds that with Goethe he often feels "too acutely: 'this is what Goethe the man believed', instead of merely entering into a world which Goethe has created; with Lucretius also; less with the Bhagavad-Gita, which is the next greatest philosophical poem to the Divine Comedy." Goethe always arouses in Eliot a "strong sense of disbelief in what he believes; Dante does not. I believe this is because Dante is the purer poet, not because I have more sympathy with Dante the man than with Goethe

[27] Baudelaire in Our Time, *Essays Ancient and Modern,* pp. 73-74. Baudelaire i.

[28] Epistle X to Can Grande.

[29] *Selected Essays,* p. 258.

[30] *Selected Essays,* p. 258.

the man."[31] [32] Maritain goes even further; he considers that the reason for this feeling lies in the very characteristics of the religious doctrine to which Dante adhered: "A coherent, traditional system of dogma and morality such as the Catholic creed remains independent of the personality that expresses it, for whoever even without faith tries to understand and to accept it." Maritain admits however that this is not true of all Catholic poets. The persuasive virtue of which Eliot speaks is due to the "native and sovereign primacy of poetic meaning over intelligible meaning. The writer's ego has disappeared in the creative Self of the poet. Theologal faith itself, the most sacred belief, has become part of the work through the instrument of creative emotion and poetic knowledge."[33]

Culture and Christianity

Basing himself on the example of Baudelaire, Eliot has realised the fact that any truly great poetry must have a moral foundation; in a word, it cannot ignore the essential problem, which is that of Good and Evil or of Original Sin. "Man is man because he can recognize supernatural realities, not because he can invent them."[34] While supporting an alliance between humanism and religion, Eliot does not believe that the humanist doctrine can in itself take the place of belief. "Our problem being to form the future, we can only form it on the materials of the past; we must use our heredity instead of denying it. The religious habits of the race are still very strong, in all places, at all times, and for all people. There is no humanistic habit; humanism is, I think, merely the state of mind of a few persons, in a few places, at a few times."[35] At a time of heresy and intellectual indiscipline, religious unity is the great factor of moral stability. 'When morals cease to be a matter of tradition and orthodoxy—that is, of the habits of the com-

[31] ibid.

[32] Eliot has revised certain of the judgments expressed in *After Strange Gods*.

[33] Eliot's basic ideas on the subject are set forth in "Religion and Literature."

[34] *Selected Essays*, p. 447.

[35] *For Lancelot Andrewes*, p. 130.

munity, formulated, corrected and elevated by the continuous thought and direction of the Church—and when each man is to elaborate his own, then *personality* becomes a thing of alarming importance."[36]

True, Eliot admits that for the poet, morals are only a secondary question, whereas for the saint they are a primary question. Yet a moral preoccupation seems to him essential in any work of art of universal significance. And that is what makes him particularly harsh towards those who, like D. H. Lawrence or André Gide, throw off all bridles, accept all natural necessities and seek to explain civilized man by primitive man. We need a faith, and literature cannot serve as a substitute for religion; for in Maritain's phrase, "it is a deadly error to expect poetry to provide the super-substantial nourishment of man". Eliot has said: "I hold the religious conception of ultimate values to be right, the humanist wrong. From the nature of things, these categories are not inevitable, like the categories of time and space, but are equally objective. In speaking of religion, it is to this level of abstraction that I wish to refer. I have none of the feelings of *nostalgia,* the reverence for tradition, the desire to recapture the sentiment of Fra Angelico, which seems to animate most modern defenders of religion. All that seems to me to be bosh. What is important, is what nobody seems to realize—the dogmas like that of Original Sin, which are the closest expression of the categories of the religious attitude. That man is in no sense perfect, but a wretched creature, who can yet apprehend perfection. It is not then that I put up with the dogma for the sake of the sentiment, but I may possibly swallow the sentiment for the sake of the dogma."[37]

* *

It is impossible to speak of Eliot without taking into account his beliefs, his constant spiritual progress, his rejection, finally,

[36] *After Strange Gods,* p. 54.
[37] *Selected Essays,* pp. 452-453.

of that spiritual pride which Pascal called "the lust of the mind". We feel that he has reflected at great length on Pascal's distinction between the *esprit de finesse* and the *esprit de géométrie;* following the moralist's advice, he acquired a clear view of the former's countless and subtle principles, and argues from these familiar principles with sound judgment, consistently and logically. Above all he has never forgotten that "the heart has its reasons, unknown to reason"; steeped in Aquinas and Maritain, he never followed the Romantics in their tendentious interpretations. He has allotted to theology the first place, which belongs to it by right. And so, basing himself on Pascal's "three orders", the order of Nature, the order of Mind and the order of Charity, he realises that "the three are discontinuous; the higher is not implicit in the lower as in an evolutionary doctrine it would be. It is true that to lead him towards Pascal Eliot had, in England, a reliable guide in the person of Newman.

Strict and impersonal as he appears, Eliot is far from being a "Monsieur Teste"; he remains inseparable from his writings; but he has shunned any sort of sentimental confession or personal outpouring; he seems to stand midway between committedness and complete freedom. He might say with Valéry: "There is no theory which is not a fragment, carefully prepared, of autobiography."

In his book of essays, *The Idea of a Christian Society,* Eliot endeavours to examine, not the faults or injustices of the society in which we live, but the very notion of it, its end. He begins by dispelling the mistaken and unfortunately widespread notions about "Western democracies" which fancy themselves part of a Christian community. Are our societies Christian because the practice of Christianity is freely allowed therein? Or should it not be said that a society ceases to be Christian when religious practice is abandoned, when religious behaviour is no longer governed by Christian principles, and when in fact prosperity becomes, for the individual or the group, the only end consciously pursued? "A society has not ceased to be Christian until it has become positively something else. It is my contention that we have today a culture which is mainly negative, but which, so far as it is positive, is still Christian. I do not think that it can remain negative, because a negative culture has ceased to be efficient in a world where economic as well as spiritual forces are proving the efficiency of cultures which, even when pagan, are positive. . ."[38]

The rejection of Pagan cultures implies the working-out of a new Christian culture. It would be wrong if in the name of democracy and liberty our opposition dwindled to a vague and ineffective antipathy towards the principles advocated by the rival forms of totalitarianism, both derived from Hegel. One might indeed reply to Eliot that what unites the "Western democracies" is not the identity of the theological foundations on which their regimes are based, even less the desire to see the Christian spirit govern them effectively; it is, none the less, undeniably a confused aspiration towards a regime of social justice in which natural rights would not be constantly infringed. The fact that these democratic regimes allow certain injustices—sometimes blatant—to subsist should not blind us to the rightness of these regimes' reaction in face of iniquities that impair the very foundations of all justice. However, when dealing with so-called Christian societies, the question that interests Eliot primarily is not that of the relations between Church and State, nor even that of the religious value of individuals in such a society; he seeks rather to introduce the spirit of the Gospel into the institutions in which Christians and non-Christians act. And if the present time inspires him with sad thoughts, his hope remains none the less keen: "The world is trying the experiment of attempting to form a civilized but non-Christian mentality. The experiment will fail; but we must be very patient in awaiting its collapse; meanwhile redeeming the time; so that the Faith may be preserved alive through the dark ages before us; to renew and rebuild civilization, and save the world from suicide."[39]

[38] If the scope of this book and the character of this series allowed it, we should have liked to study in greater detail the sociological and religious aspects of Eliot's thought.

[39] *Thoughts after Lambeth.*

BIBLIOGRAPHY

WORKS BY T. S. ELIOT

I—POETRY

Prufrock and Other Observations, The Egoist Ltd., London, 1917.
Poems, L. and V. Woolf, Hogarth Press, Richmond, 1919.
Ara Vos Prec, Ovid Press, London, 1920.
Poems, Knopf, New York, 1920.
The Waste Land, Boni and Liveright, New York, 1922.
Poems, 1909-1925, Faber and Gwyer, London, 1925.
Collected Poems, 1900-1935, Faber and Faber, London, 1936.
Old Possum's Book of Practical Cats, Faber and Faber, London, 1938.
Four Quartets, Faber and Faber, London, 1943.

II—PLAYS

The Rock, Faber and Faber, London, 1934.
Murder in the Cathedral, Faber and Faber, London, 1935.
The Family Reunion, Faber and Faber, London, 1939.
The Cocktail Party, Faber and Faber, London, 1950.
The Confidential Clerk, Faber and Faber, London, 1953.
The Elder Statesman, Faber and Faber, London, 1959.

III—ESSAYS ETC.

Ezra Pound, His Metric and Poetry, Knopf, New York, 1917.
The Sacred Wood, Methuen, London, 1920.
Homage to John Dryden, Three Essays on the Poetry of the Seventeenth Century, L. and V. Woolf, Hogarth Press, Richmond, 1924.

Shakespeare and the Stoicism of Seneca, The Shakespeare Association, Oxford University Press, 1927.

For Lancelot Andrewes, Essays on Style and Order, Faber and Gwyer, London, 1928.

Dante, Faber and Faber, London, 1929.

Thoughts After Lambeth, Faber and Faber, London, 1931.

Charles Whibley, A Memoir. The English Association Pamphlet, No. 80, Oxford University Press, 1931.

Selected Essays, Faber and Faber, London, 1932.

John Dryden, The Poet. The Dramatist. The Critic. Terence and Elsa Holliday, New York, 1932.

The Use of Poetry and the Use of Criticism. Studies in the Relation of Criticism to Poetry in England. Faber and Faber, London, 1933.

After Strange Gods. A Primer of Modern Heresy, Faber and Faber, London, 1934.

Elizabethan Essays, Faber and Faber, London, 1934.

Essays Ancient and Modern, Faber and Faber, London, 1936.

The Idea of a Christian Society, Faber and Faber, London, 1936.

Points of View, edited by John Hayward, Faber and Faber, London, 1941.

The Classics and the Man of Letters, Oxford University Press, 1942.

What is a Classic? Faber and Faber, London, 1945.

Notes towards the definition of culture, Faber and Faber, London, 1948.

To Criticize the Critic, Faber and Faber, 1965.

WORKS DEVOTED EXCLUSIVELY TO T. S. ELIOT

ANTS Oras, *The Critical Ideas of T. S. Eliot,* Tartu Esthonie, 1932.

BRAYBROOKE Neville, 1923, *T. S. Eliot, a symposium for his seventieth birthday,* New York, Farrar, Strauss and Cudahy, 1958.

DREW Elizabeth A., *T. S. Eliot, The Design of his Poetry,* New York, Scribner's Sons, 1949.

GALLUP Donald, *T. S. Eliot, a bibliography,* Faber and Faber, 1952.

GARDNER Helen, *The Art of T. S. Eliot,* London, 1949.

GREENE Edward J. H., *T. S. Eliot et la France,* thèse pour le Doctorat d'Université, présenté à la Faculté des Lettres de Paris, Edit. Contemporaines, Boivin, Paris, 1951.

GRUDIN Louis, *Mr. Eliot Among the Nightingales,* Joiner and Steele, London, and Lawrence Drake, Paris, 1932.

McGREEVY Thomas, *T. S. Eliot, A study,* Chatto and Windus, London, 1931.

MATTHIESSEN F. O., *The Achievement of T. S. Eliot,* An Essay on the Nature of Poetry, Oxford University Press, 1935.

MAXWELL D. E. S., *The Poetry of T. S. Eliot,* Routledge, 1952.

PRESTON Raymond, *Four Quartets Rehearsed,* a Commentary on T. S. Eliot's Cycle of Poems, Sheed and Ward, London, 1946.

ROBBINS Rossel Hope, *The T. S. Eliot Myth,* H. Schuman, New York, 1951.

STEPHENSON E. M., *T. S. Eliot and the Lay Reader,* Fortune Press, London, 1944.

TORDEUR Jean, *A la Rencontre de Thomas Stearns Eliot, Un Classique Vivant,* La Sixaine, Bruxelles, n. d.

UNGER Leonard, *T. S. Eliot,* Minneapolis, University of Minesota Press, 1961.

UNGER Leonard, *T. S. Eliot,* a selective critique, Noonday Press, 1953.

WILLIAMSON George, *A Reader's Guide Book to T. S. Eliot, a Poem by Poem Analysis,* The Noonday Press, New York, 1953.

T. S. Eliot, A Study in his Writings by several Hands, edited by B. Rajan, Dennis Dobson, London, 1947.

(Studies by Cleanth Brooks, E. E. Duncan-Jones, H. L. Gardner, B. Rajan, Philip Wheelwright, Anne Rider, M. C. Bradbrook, Wolf Mankovitz).

See also: "For T. S. Eliot", *The Harvard Advocate,* Advocate House, Cambridge, Mass., December 1948.

T. S. Eliot, A Symposium, compiled by Richard March and Tambimuttu, Poetry, London, 1948.

T. S. Eliot, A Selected Critique, edited by L. Unger, New York, 1949.

Other Works

Aldington Richard, *Literary Studies and Reviews,* Allen and Unwin, London, 1924.

Cattaui Georges, *Trois Poètes, Hopkins, Yeats, Eliot,* L. V. F., Paris, 1947.

Cestre Charles, *Les Poètes Américains,* Presses Universit. de France, Paris, 1948.

Curtius Ernst-Robert, *Essais sur la Littérature Européenne,* Grasset, Paris, 1954.

Fernandez Ramon, *Messages, première série,* Gallimard, Paris, 1926.

Hamilton Rostrevor, *Poetry and Contemplation,* Cambridge University Press, 1937.

Leavis F. R., *New Bearings in English Poetry,* Chatto and Windus, London, 1932.

Lewis C. Day, *A Hope for Poetry,* Basil Blackwell, Oxford, 1934.

Macneice Louis, Modern Poetry, Oxford University Press, 1938.

Maritain, Jacques, *Creative Intuition in Art and Poetry,* Harvill Press, London, 1953.

Megroz R. L., *Modern English Poetry,* 1882-1932, Ivor Nicolson and Watson, London, 1933.

Mercanton Jacques, *Poètes de l'Univers,* Skira, Geneva.

Pound Ezra, *Instigations,* Boni and Liveright, New York, 1920.

Raiziss Sona, *La Poésie Américaine Moderniste,* 1910-1940, Mercure de France, Paris, 1948.

Read Herbert, *Form in Modern Poetry,* Sheed and Ward, London, 1932.

Richards I. A., *Principles of Literary Criticism,* Kegan Paul, Trench, Trubner & Co, London, 1926.

RIDING Laura and GRAVES Robert, *A Survey of Modernist Poetry,* Heinemann, London, 1927.

ROBERTS Michael, *Critique of Poetry,* Cape 1934.

SITWELL Edith, *Aspects of Modern Poetry,* Duckworth, London, 1934.

SPARROW John, *Sense and Poetry,* Yale University Press, New Haven, 1934.

SPENDER Stephen, *The Destructive Element,* Jonathan Cape, London, 1935.

TATE Allen, *Reactionary Essays on Poetry and Ideas,* Scribner's, New York.

TAUPIN René, *L'Influence du Symbolisme français sur la Poésie Américaine,* 1910-1920, Honoré Champion, Paris, 1929.

WILLIAMS Charles, *Poetry at Present,* Clarendon Press, Oxford, 1930.

WILSON Edmund, *Axel's Castle,* Scribner's, New York, 1931.

ARTICLES

ASTRE Georges-Albert, "T. S. Eliot, poète spirituel", *Critique,* Paris, April-May 1948.

BARBOT G., "Visite à T. S. Eliot", *Gazette des Lettres,* 12 October 1946.

BEVAN I., "T. S. Eliot est maintenant un auteur à succès", *Le Figaro Littéraire,* 2 Sept. 1950.

BOLLE Louis, "L'œuvre poétique de T. S. Eliot", *La Gazette de Lausanne,* 5 June 1954.

BOWRA C. M., "T. S. Eliot, Aspects de la Littérature Anglaise", (1918-1945), Fontaine, Paris, 1947.

BRION Marcel, "T. S. Eliot, Prix Nobel", *Revue des Deux Mondes,* 1949.

CURTIUS Ernst-Robert, "T. S. Eliot als Dichter", *Neue Schweizer Rundschau* (32-33), 1927, pp. 349-361.

CURTIUS Ernst-Robert, "T. S. Eliot als Kritiker", *Die Literatur,* Oct. 1929. pp. 11-15, 1944.

HAUSERMANN H. W., "L'Œuvre Poétique de T. S. Eliot", *Le Mois Suisse,* 1944.

LABOULLE M. J. J., "T. S. Eliot and some French Poets", *Revue de Littérature Comparée,* April-June 1936, p. 389.

MIRSKY D. S., "T. S. Eliot et la fin de la Poésie Bourgeoise", *Echanges,* December 1931.

MELCHIORI Giorgio, "The Lotus and the Rose, D. H. Lawrence, T. S. Eliot, Four Quartets", *English Miscellany.*

MURRY J. Middleton, "The Return of the Mayflower", *New Adelphi,* March-May 1929.

McCARTHY Desmond, "The Work of T. S. Eliot", *Sunday Times,* 3 Nov. 1933.

NIMR Amy, "Introduction à la Poésie de T. S. Eliot", *Echanges,* March 1931.

PRAZ Mario, "T. S. Eliot", *L'Italia che Scrive,* Oct. 1956.

ROUSSEAUX André, "La Poésie de T. S. Eliot", *Le Figaro Littéraire,* 27th December 1947.

TODD Olivier, "T. S. Eliot contre l'Humain", *Les Temps Modernes.*

TURNELL G. M., "Introduction to the Study of Tristan Corbière", *Criterion,* April 1936.

WAHL Jean, "Poems, 1909-1925" (Compte rendu), *Nouvelle Revue Française,* April 1933.